EXITING THE MAZE

Professor Malley,

Thank you for the opportunity
to speak to your class.
May God bless you with His
peace and joy always.

EXITING THE MAZE

NATHAN COLE

ISBN 978-0-9891367-2-3 Softcover
ISBN 978-0-9891367-3-0 ebook

Published by Next Level Press, a division of Complxx, Inc.
www.nextlevelpress.net

Unless otherwise identified, Scripture quotations are taken from the
King James Version of the Holy Bible.

All emphasis in the Scripture quotations is the author's.

Contents

Dedication

God, everything I am, I owe to You.
This is Your story, and it belongs to You.
For the rest of my life, I give it all to You.

I am writing this book because God has worked a powerful testimony in my life over the past few years, and I want to share it with others. I am forever grateful for what He has done, and I pray that my journey serves as a witness to God's power to deliver and transform lives.

To every individual struggling with fear, anxiety, or any other form of bondage—there is hope!
And that hope is in Christ Jesus.

Foreword

We are privileged, through the pages of this book, to be masterfully guided by Nathan Cole as he travels through the dark valley of obsessive-compulsive disorder to the mountain peak of liberty and true freedom. In my judgment, Nathan's empirical, precious life experience serves as a testimonial and witness to the unconditional love and power of God found in Christ Jesus.

My ministry career of over 25 years has afforded me the opportunity to interface with thousands of people. The common thread that appears to be pervasive throughout the whole of humanity is the need and desire to be whole. Unfortunately, a great number of people have learned to function sufficiently in one area of life while languishing severely crippled in another. Nathan, an erudite, brilliant University of Michigan graduate, displays in this book the paradox of the superlative cohabiting with the discombobulated.

The worlds of psychology and law enforcement continue to grapple with how people of great promise and potential can suddenly lose control and descend into madness. This riveting story's promise is to provide us with a view into the mind of some of society's most mysterious characters. Nathan's journey to wholeness shines a radiant light on some of our most perplexing social ills. His journey also seems to metaphorically parallel Dorothy's attempt to find her way home in the epic tale *The Wizard of Oz*. Like Dorothy, Nathan comes full circle to realize that the truth he sought at a distance was as close to him as his next breath.

I believe the compelling insight contained within this book will inspire the hearts of many to pursue wellness as a way of life. I therefore recommend this book not only to those challenged with OCD, but to anyone who wants to know authentic freedom and a peace that passes all understanding.

Hugh D. Smith Jr.

Senior Pastor, Embassy Covenant Church International
National Bishop, Jabula New Life International - USA

Introduction:
The Exit Strategy

The lights were low in the sanctuary, the worship band was playing, and people all around me were praying. My friends seemed to be experiencing God in powerful ways, but I sat in the pew, lost in confusion. I could not escape the mental torment that had become my reality. I was trying to find God, but my mind had been imprisoned for a long time. As I struggled through the endless twists and turns of delusional thinking, a friend of mine came and sat next to me.

I shared my frustration with him: "I feel like I'm lost in a maze...a confusing maze of thoughts...and I cannot find the exit."

He responded in a reassuring voice: "Sometimes, Nathan, the only way **out** is **up**."

*****

I am writing this book because God miraculously delivered me from obsessive-compulsive disorder (OCD). Although I grew up in a Christian home, I eventually exalted my own intellect above anything I deemed to be "spiritual." Simultaneously, I found myself grappling increasingly with irrational, paralyzing fear. I darted anxiously through dark, twisted psychological mazes, lost in torment and confusion.

But God healed me. His light pierced the darkness, and He rescued me from myself. God loved me, comforted me, and ultimately, He renewed my mind.

In some ways, my journey thus far has been about learning how to look up — to turn to God in the midst of madness — and I have experienced the profound peace that comes from exalting God above every quandary and complexity.

Interestingly, one particular story from the Bible seems to bear a striking resemblance to my own, at least in terms of deliverance from mental bondage. Many years ago, during the Babylonian Captivity of the Jewish people, King Nebuchadnezzar surveyed his glorious kingdom. He strutted about his palace, proclaiming his own greatness: "Is not this great Babylon, that I have built for the house of the kingdom by the might of my power, and for the honour of my majesty?" (Daniel 4:30).

Lifted up in pride, the king refused to recognize the true and living God, so God fulfilled a prophetic word and struck the king with madness. God stripped King Nebuchadnezzar of his kingdom. The dethroned king was driven from among men, and his dwelling was made with the beasts of the field. He ate grass like an ox, and his body was wet with the dew of heaven. His insanity plagued him until his hair was "grown like eagles' feathers, and his nails like birds' claws" (Daniel 4:33).

Finally, after a lengthy season of mental torment, the king looked **up** to heaven and blessed God, recognizing Him as the only One with all power and all authority. King Nebuchadnezzar's understanding and reason returned to him, and he continued to bless the most High God. His kingdom was restored, and excellent majesty was added to him.

The king had learned by experience who was in charge: "Now I Nebuchadnezzar praise and extol and honour the King of heaven, all whose works are truth, and his ways judgment: and those that walk in pride he is able to abase" (Daniel 4:37).

Never in my life did I think that I would be able to identify with this story from the Old Testament, but God works in mysterious ways. Like King Nebuchadnezzar, God allowed me to struggle severely with a mental disorder for a season. In the end, however, He healed me, and I finally knew within myself that He was the true and living God.

If not for the grace of God, I could easily be in a mental institution right now, but God saw fit to save me. I am a living witness to God's power to restore a person's mind, and my hope is that my testimony will be a source of encouragement and inspiration for others. There are so many people who suffer with various mental conditions and disorders. Some of their experiences may be less severe than mine, and some may be even more severe, but in the end, God is the Healer.

As believers, we do not have to struggle with debilitating anxiety. We do not have to live our lives in fear, guilt, and shame. Jesus Christ paid the price on the cross so that we can have freedom, and He has freely given His peace to all those who put their faith in Him.

Not only did God lead me out of the darkness, but He brought me into the light. The level of peace that I experience in my life now would not have been possible just a few years ago, but thanks to God, I am now able to enjoy life, love, and joy in ways that I previously could not. That same grace from God is available to everyone. Nothing is impossible with our God. Nothing is impossible if we can only look **up**.

CHAPTER
1

Binding Every Thought

Casting down imaginations, and every high thing that
exalteth itself against the knowledge of God, and bringing
into captivity every thought to the obedience of Christ
(2 Corinthians 10:5)

I first learned the value of thought from Bishop Hugh D. Smith
Jr., a spiritual father who has since become one of the most influential
people in my life. I was in 8th grade, and I had never before heard a
preacher with so much insight and revelatory knowledge. I scribbled
page after page of notes during his sermon, a practice which my Mom
was grateful that I had finally taken up again.

My family had driven an hour to church that day to hear Bishop
Smith, and it was worth it. He spoke of "binding every thought" and
bringing it into captivity to the obedience of Christ. Thoughts create
realities, and Bishop Smith shared the importance of properly governing the mind. Little did I know then how important that idea would
become.

I was always analytical, even as a child, and this often got me into
trouble with those in positions of authority. I would notice logical in-

consistencies and, lacking wisdom, would point them out indiscriminately. My mind was very active, and I found myself constantly questioning and reasoning my way through various ideas and arguments. To put it simply, I was (and I still am) a critical thinker.

When I first heard Bishop Smith speak about "binding every thought," I took it very literally, and instead of a life-enhancing spiritual principle, it slowly became a tormenting obsession. I attempted to annihilate every fleeting thought that I deemed to be sinful. I would recite a prayer of repentance after each thought, and as soon as I would conclude the prayer, another thought would come, and I had to start the process all over again.

As a middle schooler, I felt like I was in a battle, a constant and unyielding spiritual struggle, and I was a soldier fighting off demonic forces. Perhaps it was this experience that inspired me to write a fairly lengthy poem entitled "War of the Mind." I will not reproduce the entire work, but these few verses should suffice to provide a sense of the poem's content:

> I survey the battlefield, the realm of the mind.
> I guard against every ill thought that I find.
>
> I grip my sword with steady hands,
> Prepared to fight the demonic lands.
>
> Legions are amassed to bring death and sin,
> But against this authority, they cannot win.

I see a thought coming, gruesome and sick.
I raise up my shield, and swing my blade quick.

My saber I pierce through its defiled chest.
In the fires of hell it shall find no rest.

For hours it seems is the battle drawn out,
But I won't give in, and I will not doubt.

The armies have subsided, delivered unto death.
I begin to fatigue, I'm all out of breath.

Lord, give me strength and fill me with praise.
Let me be in your will and follow your ways.

These words were a fairly accurate description of what I was experiencing at the time. The cyclical process of fighting each individual thought was ultimately exhausting. After perhaps several hours of
unrelenting struggle, I would be psychologically drained. I remember
curling up on my parents' bed, tears flowing, crying out because of the
mental torment. They prayed earnestly for me, confirmed their love,
and I felt a measure of relief.

I also remember thinking thoughts that, in retrospect, can only be
described as obsessive-compulsive. One night, I was lying in my bed
trying to go to sleep, but I could not find any rest. My parents had instructed me to keep my room clean, which was fine, except that from
my bed I could see a small piece of black lint on the light-colored car-

peting. It bothered me; I felt like I had a moral obligation to pick it up.

On some level, I probably knew how silly that was, but I felt compelled to do it anyway. Leaving it on the floor would leave me with the weight of a guilty conscience. Similar thoughts plagued me throughout the day: small, minute details were blown out of proportion and became sources of psychological stress.

I was terrified of making a mistake. The fear of sinning against God was almost unbearable, and guilt and shame found a gateway into my life. After one particularly difficult day, I came to my Dad, trying to find a solution to what I was struggling with. He reminded me that "God's grace is sufficient," and he instructed me to recite that phrase before I went to sleep at night—to let go of all other thoughts and just rest, trusting God.

The thought of God's grace was precisely what I needed to hear, but the thought often became twisted in my mind, just like everything else. Sometimes it would work; other times, it became just one more phrase that I repeated repetitiously, and my mind would dissolve it into the rest of the confusion. Eventually, I would come to experience the true grace and love of God in a life-transforming way, but at this juncture, I was only at the beginning of a long and arduous journey toward rediscovering God.

CHAPTER
2

I Got a Question...

Beware lest any man spoil you through philosophy and
vain deceit, after the tradition of men, after the rudi-
ments of the world, and not after Christ
(Colossians 2:8)

Fast forward to the summer before college. High school had been
a whole lot of fun. Although it was an emotional roller coaster ride in
many ways, I walked away with an amazing group of friends and some
incredible experiences. I played violin for an award-winning orchestra
that traveled the country, went to Mexico a couple times on mission
trips with a Chinese youth ministry, and asked a beautiful girl to my
first Homecoming dance. On top of it all, I pulled off a perfect 4.0
GPA. It was a good four years.

The summer after high school graduation was filled with hangouts,
grad parties, and soaking up the sun with good friends. As college drew
near though, I began to become a bit more apprehensive. For whatever
reason, I began to expect an "intellectual onslaught" against my faith.
Earlier that summer, a youth pastor had given me and several others a
copy of *How to Stay Christian in College* by J. Budziszewski. I think I

read some of it, and perhaps it got me thinking about the challenges ahead. On August 21, 2007, I wrote the following:

> I've been a bit worried about college lately...the attacks that will be made on my faith, the intellectual onslaught. I don't want to doubt my beliefs. I've been scared for myself and for my brothers and sisters [in Christ]. I'm definitely going to need God's help with this one...Lord God, keep me close to you. Please don't allow my faith to waver. Let me only grow stronger, I pray. Give me a good support system. Make my faith real and unshakable! I love you, Father.

Several days later, the struggle had not relented. I had questioned various aspects of my faith before, but this time was different:

> Recently, my doubts have started to scare me. My analytical mind keeps challenging what I believe, and I hate it. I want to be able to simply believe...with no doubt in my mind or in my heart. I want an unshakable faith in God and in the truth of his Word. I want to know the truth so that I can be free of this inner turmoil. I'm calling into question the very foundation of my life, and it's really frightening me. God, if you could just help me [get] past this test...

The next day, I arrived on the University of Michigan campus in Ann Arbor, Michigan. My family came with me to help me move into my Baits II dorm room on North Campus. My roommate had not yet arrived, and Bishop Smith and one of his daughters came by to pray with us in the room. It was a bittersweet moment: as my family said their final teary-eyed goodbyes, I tasted independence for the first time—but simultaneously realized how alone I felt without them.

Despite the initial loneliness, however, a whole new world opened up to me, and I dove right in. I began to explore various churches with my friends and finally landed at Harvest Mission Community Church (HMCC), a tremendous ministry that I participated in throughout my college career. As a part of my religious quest at the time, I took a World Religions course during my first semester that explored the three "Abrahamic" faiths: Judaism, Christianity, and Islam. Far from confirming my Christian theological understandings, this course brought ever more questions to a mind already fraught with doubt.

On September 10, just days into my college experience, I emailed my Mom to let her know about the doubts that I was grappling with. It was a difficult move for me because I was unsure how things would unfold after I revealed that I was questioning my faith at that level. I'll share part of that email. Here, I confess:

> ...What's becoming pretty common, though, is challenges to my faith. My English professor spoke almost mockingly about the idea that the Bible is the direct "Word of God." My Psychology textbook states that for one to understand the basic principles of psychology one must accept that everything has a physical cause, that any supernatural part of man is of no importance in the field, and that the human mind is a product of the biological means of natural selection as stated by Charles

Darwin. In my [World] Religions textbook, I often detect a subtle, underlying anti-Christian tone. I've talked/debated with an agnostic friend twice now about God, morality, and truth.

All of this wouldn't be so bad...if it weren't for the doubts in my own mind about my faith. If you looked at my journal right now, you would find that it's filled with frustration, mostly at myself. I want so badly to just simply believe what I've been taught and what I have experienced in my life. But my mind keeps sending me through tormenting mental gymnastics every single day. I keep questioning: "Who am I to say I have absolute truth when I've experienced nothing else?" "Are all my 'experiences' just emotional?" "How do I prove that Christianity is real?" "Is my Psychology book really right? Is my concept of God just a function of my brain?" "Is my [World] Religions book right? Is the Bible tainted with the views of biased writers?"

I desperately want to know the truth. I need God to confirm within me once again the reality of His existence, His word, His sacrifice on the cross... I want to believe! I don't want to doubt! I hate my doubts, and I'm ashamed of them. But I can't seem to shake them off or get rid of them. And this isn't just because of college. I wrestled with this even before I left.

I feel like such a failure as a Christian. How can God use me? I've been trained for 18 years, and I'm still grappling with the basics? I shouldn't be struggling. It's not like I'm in a completely spiritually dead environment. I mean, Harvest is really good. The worship, the messages...it's just me.

...You said to tell you if I needed prayer. Well, I'm taking you up on that. Please pray for me, Mom. I need it. It took a lot just to say all that.

I love you. And thank you.

I'm sure that my email created a few shock waves, but after a brief moment of intense concern, my Mom prayed about the situation, and God reassured her. Later on, she will share her story about that experience in her own words.

Bishop Smith called a few days later to check up on me and encourage me. I suppose my Mom had mentioned to him my doubts about my faith. He assured me that it was normal to go through a season of questioning everything. I was becoming a man, and I needed to know things for myself. He told me that I would make the right choice in the end and that I would be a stronger believer once I had gone through this. His words were comforting, and I felt better for a little while.

During this season, I discovered a Scripture that perfectly described how I felt: wanting so desperately to believe but feeling unable to shake the doubts. In the story, a father brings his possessed son to Jesus, seeking deliverance. "Jesus said unto him, If thou canst believe, all things are possible to him that believeth. And straightway the father of the child cried out, and said with tears, Lord, I believe; help thou mine unbelief" (Mark 9:23-24).

First, he tells Jesus that he believes. Then, seemingly in the same breath, he asks Jesus to help him with his unbelief. The paradox of the father's statement resonated with me. I knew exactly how he felt. I remember one night in particular, lying on my dorm room bed at night, looking up at the ceiling. Tears were flowing because I just wanted to praise God, but I felt so lost, not even sure if He was there anymore... or if He ever was.

I felt as if the foundation that I had been standing on for my entire life had suddenly disappeared. There was nothing to grab ahold of, nothing to hang onto. I was floating in an endless space without coherence, purpose, or meaning. The truth upon which I had built my reality was being fundamentally challenged, and it was difficult to bear.

What do you do when the very ground upon which you stand is pulled out from underneath you? I pored through the Scriptures, looking for answers. On one occasion, I flipped through every page of the Four Gospels in one sitting, searching for an instance in which Jesus had explicitly and indisputably claimed to be God. I researched and analyzed Isaiah 58—was it really a Messianic prophecy or just a reference to the nation of Israel? Questions abounded, and answers were scarce.

Another journal entry, this one from November 14, 2007, provides a window into the deluge of questions that were springing up:

> Muslims have faith just like we do. They have similar emotional experiences, as well. What separates them from us? If there isn't any proof for Christianity, if it must be accepted by faith, how would anybody know which religion to have faith in? I could say I believe in Christianity just because it feels right and there seems to be enough truth in it to give it a try. But then, wouldn't I have to try everything, then, if I were to make the best decision possible? Muslims believe in God just

as much as we do. They believe they are worshipping the one true God. Who are we to say that they are not?

Who is Jesus? What is the role of the Messiah in the Jewish tradition? Which scriptures are considered to be Messianic prophecies? Why was there no concept of a "second coming" until Christianity? Why are there so many discrepancies between Jews and Christians on these issues?

What is truth? That is an excellent question. I used to think that Pilate was just stupid or something, but the question is extremely valid.

Why, when I ask God to reveal himself to me, do I leave feeling so empty?

Does it take more faith to believe in God or not to believe in him?

Is love just a psychological result of natural selection for the purposes of survival and reproduction? Is every act of apparent altruism inherently selfish in the end?

If there is no God, does anything really matter at all? Would there be any purpose to life?

How are we so sure that there is only one God? How are we so sure that there is nothing above our God?

The simple faith that I see in others...is it just ignorance? What does it take to believe? Faith comes by hearing, and hearing by the Word of God. I need to hear from you, Lord Jesus. I need to hear something that I know is not me. Please talk to my spirit, I pray.

Am I just a failure? God, can you raise the dead in me?

Why does it seem like I can't reach you without music? Doesn't that just add to the idea that this is all just an emotional experience?

"My God, my God, why have you forsaken me?" Or have I forsaken you? Either way, I need help.

As I continued to go to church, go to class, and go out with friends, I continued to muse. I had opened the floodgates, and the thoughts and questions kept coming. November 23, 2007:

I believe in love. And if God is love, then I believe in God. Sometimes I don't even know what the heck I'm saying. Or if what I'm saying is the truth. Sometimes I find it really hard to understand faith. How am I supposed to just believe something without really knowing it? Why has this become so hard?

...Christianity. The only religion where we are saved by faith, by grace. The only religion where God sacrifices himself to save us. Man is so wretched. How could we possibly save ourselves? How could we possibly deliver ourselves? If salvation was based on works, I think we would all go to hell. We cannot do it alone. It must take God's grace. A religion with love as its foundation.

If there is no God, then why does belief in God seem so natural sometimes? Why does worship feel so right? Why do I feel so fulfilled when I believe? Perhaps others are not struggling with the answers because they are not asking the questions.

"In the chaos, in confusion, I know you're sovereign still."
– Hillsong United

I long for quiet, for stillness. I long for peace within my soul, an assurance of the truth. I want to hear the voice of God within my spirit. I want to whisper back to him. ...I want a relationship with God, a belief in God that goes beyond music, beyond emotion. Maybe trying to intellectualize God is like trying to imagine a dimension above us. It is simply beyond our ability to comprehend, no matter how hard we try. And yet...

2 Timothy 3:7 "Ever learning, and never able to come to the knowledge of the truth."

I was profoundly confused, but amidst the darkness, there were glimmers of hope. In early December, I ran into a friend of mine at the Hatcher Graduate Library. We started to talk about my struggles with faith. I told him that I just really needed something that would prove God to me within myself. "So you need God to just smack you over the head?" he asked.

I laughed. "Yeah, exactly." After a while, I got up to leave, but before I got very far, my friend called me back. I sat down, and he proceeded to smack the back of my head. "That's from God," he said.

I remember cold winter days, sinking into a chair in the reading room at the graduate library, one of the most silent, scholarly places on campus. I curled up with *Mere Christianity*, a discussion and defense of Christianity by the great C.S. Lewis. The arguments in the book were, in my opinion, brilliantly composed.

C.S. Lewis was masterful: "If I find in myself a desire which no experience in this world can satisfy, the most probable explanation is that I was made for another world." Beautiful theological prose. However, I still saw holes in his statements. After all, perhaps the human need for a Higher Power could be explained at a psychological level. What if the "god" that satisfies us is unconsciously our own creation?

I simply did not understand faith. December 16, 2007:

> Sometimes I feel like God is asking the impossible. How can he expect anyone to believe in Him without any concrete proof of his existence? Faith, yes, I know. But if we don't know for sure, what right do we have to tell others what the truth is? ...An even scarier idea...what makes good "good" and evil "evil"? Is God "right" and "good" simply because he is the most powerful being? It's all so very confusing.

On Christmas Eve of that year, my mind was still traversing the realms of uncertainty:

> There's no way to prove that there's a God; there's also no way to prove that there isn't a God. So what the heck is humanity supposed to do? I'm having trouble finding any reason to believe in God at this point. Why even search for something that cannot be proven? God, if you're real, where are you?

"Where are You?" That was the million dollar question.

Incidentally, this was also the very first question that God ever asked humanity—the first "missionary call," if you will. After the Fall in the Garden of Eden, God called out for Adam, and ever since that day, God has been trying to renew his fellowship with humanity.

But I didn't feel like God was looking for me. I was looking for Him, and it seemed like I could not find Him. If there was one song that expressed the cry of my heart during my freshman year of college, it was "Silence" by Jars of Clay. I listened to that song many times that year. Here is what it said:

Take
Take till there's nothing
Nothing to turn to
Nothing when you get through
Won't you break
Scattered pieces of all I've been
Bowing to, all I've been
Running to
Where are you?
Where are you?

Did you leave me unbreakable?
You leave me frozen?
I've never felt so cold
I thought you were silent
And I thought you left me
For the wreckage and the waste
On an empty beach of faith
Was it true?

'Cause I...I got a question

I got a question

Where are you?

Scream

Deeper I wanna scream

I want you to hear me

I want you to find me

'Cause I...I want to believe

But all I pray is wrong

And all I claim is gone

And I...I got a question

I got a question

Where are you?

Yeah....yeah

And where...I...I got a question

I got a question

Where are you?

Where are you?

Where are you?

Where are you?

That is how I felt. "Where are You, God?" I was searching, but I felt like God was not responding. I remember one day in particular—I kneeled down at my bedside and cried out to God: "I need to know that You are there. I need something...I need to feel You right now."

I waited...and I felt nothing. Just emptiness, void. I could not believe it—had God really abandoned me?

The pain and shock of that moment went straight to my core. I had felt rejection from people before, but at that moment, I felt like God had rejected me. If He was real, He wanted nothing to do with me. He wouldn't answer me. I got up, and my heart was broken. What do you do when you feel like God Himself doesn't want you?

CHAPTER
3

Church Boy

I was a church boy from the very beginning. My mother went to church while she was pregnant with me, which means I was actually in the house of God long before I saw the light of day in the hospital on April 9, 1989.

As God would have it, I was born on a Sunday morning, and my parents named me Nathan, which means "God has given." When I was three years old, I quoted the titles of nearly all sixty-six books of the Bible in order—Old and New Testaments—on television. I cannot say that I remember the experience, but I watched it on videotape when I was older. Both of my parents were leaders in the church, so essentially, I grew up a "double PK" (PK = Pastor's Kid).

Raised in a predominantly African American apostolic church in Highland Park, Michigan, I was inundated with doctrinal teachings about repentance and baptism, and at the age of six, I was baptized.

Having attended Sunday School and talked with my parents, I understood the basic Gospel message: Jesus died for my sins, and through Him, I could be saved. I then received my first Communion and "tarried" at the altar to receive the gift of the Holy Ghost, evidenced by speaking in other tongues.

In 8th grade, I became the Co-President of our middle school Bible Study, and that same year, a good friend of mine invited me to a Chinese youth group called O@sis. On my first visit, I was blown away. I had never seen young people my age who were so passionate about worship. I saw people raising their hands and bowing down before God without any shame. I felt inspired, so I participated for the next several years.

Also in middle school, my parents felt that God was calling our family to transition out of the church that we were attending. We connected with Bishop Smith, who had recently launched his second ministry—this one in Ann Arbor—and eventually, my parents became part of a church plant team that launched a new ministry under the leadership of Bishop Smith in Troy, Michigan, called Embassy Covenant Church International.

I watched this ministry grow from small prayer meetings in our basement, to Bible Studies at my Dad's workplace, to our first Sunday morning service on February 1, 2004. Several years later, the church membership was around 400 people.

After my junior year of high school, I went on my first mission trip to Mexico with a small team of friends from O@sis. It was my first time outside the country (other than brief trips to Canada), and the experience changed my life forever. We participated in service projects, put together programs for children in rural towns, and shared our testimonies in local churches.

I felt completely and totally alive, and I experienced a life that was full of joy and meaning every single day.

In a small way, I was giving my life for something greater than myself. At the end of the trip, we came back to Juarez for a church service. As the band sang "Yo Te Busco," I kneeled down before the altar at the front of the church, and with tears in my eyes, I promised God that I would go wherever He sent me. I had felt the power of His love like never before, and I would go anywhere and do anything for Him.

I learned at least three major lessons from that first trip to Mexico that fundamentally shaped my worldview. First, my eyes were opened to the rest of the world in an unprecedented way. There really was a big world out there, one that was much bigger than the United States. There were other cultures, other languages, and other living conditions.

I had seen poverty in Detroit before, but the level of poverty that I saw in Mexico was shocking, and my innate sense of justice was rocked. I saw broken-down stone houses, trash scattered everywhere, and small children with tattered clothing playing in the dirt.

I found myself wondering, "How can we live so comfortably in America when just a few miles below us, people are suffering so much lack?" As we flew over Texas on the way back home, I looked down and saw McDonald's and Walmart. I thought about the hundreds of brands of toothpaste we have to choose from. I thought about the excessive opulence of American culture, and on some level, it sickened me.

Yet, for all of what I perceived to be "poverty" in Mexico, I met people who were so much richer in joy than many people I had met in America, though they had fewer material possessions. That was the second lesson—money alone cannot bring happiness. These people had next to nothing, yet their spirits exuded an inner joy that money could never buy. Some of the poorest people have the biggest smiles, and some of the richest people are the most miserable. So then, at the end of the day, who is wealthier?

Finally, I learned that the Body of Christ is a global family that transcends all barriers of culture, race, ethnicity, and language. As we said goodbye to some of our Mexican friends at Rio Chico, one of the young guys shook my hand, and with a big smile, he said, "Hermano," which means "brother."

Something clicked for me in that moment. He and I did not speak the same language, yet there was something bigger that united us: our love for Jesus Christ. The Holy Spirit had united our spirits together, and through God, we were all a part of one family. At the church in Juarez, a man put his hands on my head and began to pray in Spanish. I could not understand the words that he was saying, but I felt the power of his prayer for me. God was so much greater than our different cultures; we were more the same than we were different.

In my senior year, I served as the President of REACH (Relationships Established Around Christ's Hope), our high school Bible Study, and after graduation, I went back to Mexico on another mission trip, reconnecting with some of the same individuals and attempting to fan the flames that had been kindled in me the previous year. I did not realize it then, but when I came back to the States, I would enter the most intense trial of my life thus far.

CHAPTER
4

For What Reason?

Given my profoundly Christian upbringing, it was somewhat shocking (or perhaps not) that I found myself questioning my faith at this fundamental level in college. To say the least, this was a significant bend in my journey, and it seemed to throw me entirely off course.

At the beginning of 2008, Harvest Mission Community Church (HMCC) hosted an out-of-town church retreat, and I decided to attend. I went with a mindset that said, "God, if You don't meet me at this retreat, if I don't feel something from You, then it's over. I won't be a Christian anymore. I can no longer claim to be a part of this faith when I don't really know what I believe."

The retreat came and went, and I was still unconvinced. I sat down at my computer in my dorm room the day that we got back, logged into my Facebook account, and found the place where it said "Religious Views" on my profile page. The word "Christian" stared back at me. I clicked the button to edit the page, and I deleted it. My "Religious Views" were now gone. It may seem silly, but this was a painful, watershed moment for me. When I deleted the word "Christian," I felt like I had lost a piece of my identity.

For some reason, though, I was still going to church, reading my Bible, and trying to figure out God. I wrote many journal entries during that time, but I will only highlight a few that were significant. February 12, 2008:

> If your friend was drowning, wouldn't you save him? If he was holding a gun to his head, ready to pull the trigger, wouldn't you wrestle it away from him? As a real friend, wouldn't you rescue him, whether he wanted to be rescued or not? Wouldn't you do what was best for him, even if it wasn't what he wanted?
>
> God doesn't seem to operate this way. If you want to drown, he lets you drown. He doesn't come to rescue you if you don't want to be rescued. If you want to commit spiritual suicide, it seems like God just "respects your wishes" and watches you blow your brains out. How is this real friendship? What if I don't have the strength to make the leap of faith? Shouldn't God save me anyway, despite myself?
>
> Thomas doubted, and Jesus gave him proof. Why won't he do that for me? The eleven disciples saw Jesus physically alive after his death. Have I? Paul saw a shining light and heard a booming voice from heaven. He was knocked off his horse, blinded, and healed. Can I say the same? What reason do I have to believe?

Why the heck does anyone trust [the Bible]? To my knowledge, we don't have any of the complete original manuscripts. All we have are copies, perhaps copies of copies. Rife with errors and redundancies. Jesus spoke in Hebrew and Aramaic. The New Testament was written in Greek. We read it now in English. How much was lost in translation? Mark and Luke were not even one of the twelve disciples. The gospels are attributed to certain authors, but were perhaps constructions of entire communities. Canonization...why these books and not others? What about the Gospel of Thomas? Wasn't he one of the twelve? Why do we trust Paul so much? So much of our faith and practice is based on his words. How do we know that his interpretation of Jesus is correct? Why is he in the Bible? He's not God! Who decided that the Revelation of John was divinely inspired? Blood, fire, and destruction...is this not "hallucinatory violence"?

Most Christians blindly accept the validity of the Bible on the authority of present church leaders and past councils. Some human being made a decision to give these sixty-six books a binding and two covers. Do you trust him? Do you even know who he is?

Two days later:

There's got to be more to God, more to Christ than Christianity. If his presence is really that amazing and undeniable, how could I have fallen away into doubts and questions and confusion? ...If God is so life-changing, why do we need other people to keep telling us to make sure we believe? ...[God] has been a subject of study by theologians and philosophers and intellectuals for centuries. How can you possibly think that you've got it all figured out? That your way is right and the others wrong? Who are _you_? Of all the "revelations" in human history, what makes yours any more valid?

Say that there is a distinction between good and evil. How is good defined? How is evil defined? Why choose good over evil? Why is peace inherently better than torment? Why be "better" at all? What if evil is really good, and good really evil? Do we prefer good because God is good and he's just the biggest thing out there? Who made "biggest" best? And why be the best? This may seem foolish...but why not be foolish? Do we choose good simply because it's more comfortable?

...If God knew that millions of people would burn in the everlasting torment of hell, why did he create them? Is this a loving God? Sure, maybe Jesus rescues us if we believe in him, but God created us as creatures prone to sin in the first place!

...Not being able to disprove the existence of God is not enough reason to believe in Him. I could believe in invisible UFOs from Mars that only I can see and you couldn't disprove me. But then, by the same token, perhaps not being able to prove the existence of God is not enough reason to reject Him. What, then, is the deciding factor? Faith? But faith in what? And for what reason?

If you open yourself up to blind belief in the unseen, who

knows where you could end up? There are so many things that you could choose to believe in. Why Jesus? Is Christianity the religion that just seems to fit your morals and your worldview the best? Maybe the real truth is harsher. Which one of us knows anything? And why the need to know?

...I want to touch the scars. I want to feel the places where I hammered the nails. I want to be completely broken, to weep before the feet of my Savior. To realize my unworthiness, my spiritual bankruptcy, my betrayal. If you could save me, Lord... please save me. Please help me, Lord Jesus.

February 18, 2008:

"It is only in the mysterious equations of love that any logic or reason can be found" (*A Beautiful Mind*). Perhaps Christianity, or the model of Jesus, has so much sway over the human psyche because it seems to demonstrate perfectly the concept of unconditional love. Perhaps its power lies not in its factual basis but in the truth that one ascribes to it. Whether or not this figure even existed, the story of Jesus is so powerful for Christians for they believe it to be both fact and ultimate truth.

Can one, while in search of ultimate truth, effectively select an interim course of action or way of living? Whether or not this Truth, this Way, exists, can one live a life with love as its primary philosophy or foundation? Will this determination not ultimately fail, for what upholds it?

Pure altruism, willing self-sacrifice, seems to fulfill the necessities of both autonomy and heteronomy. Is unconditional love, then, the ultimate truth? Is this not the way of Christ? Does it go beyond Christ?

Is Jesus just a reference point, a symbolic indicator of a more transcendent truth which goes beyond the literal person? Is our conception of "God" merely a human attempt to identify the unidentifiable, to define the indefinable? Does not language limit meaning? Does not religion put Truth in a box? ...Can some form of Christian philosophy be truth without the prerequisite of factual history?

...Is it just for God to relegate to each of us an eternal state that is based solely on the actions of one human lifetime? It seems so unbalanced. Can the mysteries of the universe and God and the meaning of human life be unraveled in eighty years?

...A complexity beyond all complexities,
A simplicity beyond all simplicities,
A pure singularity, a mystery,
An unknown, a Creator.

On Good Friday of that year, HMCC held a special service to remember the sacrifice of Jesus Christ on the cross. Near the end of the service, the bread and the wine were distributed for Communion. I had taken Communion since I was a child, but for the first time in my life, I let it pass me by. I could not partake. I was not a Christian.

Something inside me broke all over again. I sat in my seat, put my face at my knees, and covered my head, crying. I loved Jesus, and I could not seem to bear the idea that I had rejected Him. It was paradoxical, to say the least: I loved God; I was just not sure He existed.

CHAPTER
5

The Devil's in the Details

My sophomore year at the University of Michigan was no easier than the previous one. The four month summer vacation had not resolved any of my issues, and I continued to struggle with fundamental uncertainties regarding my identity and my beliefs. However, this year was a bit different. I was not asking the same questions that I had asked during my freshman year.

At some point, the zeal to find the answers was replaced by disillusionment and despair. The questions had become too numerous. Before I could resolve one issue, the next one would pop up. Layers upon layers of unanswered questions were eventually stacked higher than my ability to discern between them, and ultimately, I resigned myself to the confusion that had become my reality. For the most part, I was no longer attempting to critically dissect any of these issues; I had given up the search.

I also noticed that some of my behaviors were becoming increasingly obsessive. I now lived in an 8th floor South Quad dorm room on Central Campus with Jesse, one of my closest friends. Due to our different schedules, I was often alone in the room as I went to sleep at night. Before climbing into bed, I would turn off the light. Then I would turn it back on. Then off again. Then on. Then off. Then on. Then off.

For some reason, I thought that I had to turn the light off the "right" way, and every time I got it wrong, I had to do it again. Sometimes, I wondered what the people on the other side of the building must have thought when they saw the glow from our room go on and off like a blinking Christmas tree light. Perhaps my mind had connected the act of turning the light off with something more sinister, like ending someone's life, and I was trying desperately to shake the associated image. Perhaps my mind was just stuck. Whatever the case, it was a compulsion that seemed impossible to ignore.

Other behaviors were equally strange. At times, I found myself jumping slightly off the ground whenever I had a sinful thought, as if landing on the ground again would give me a fresh start. I began to cough or tense up my body repetitively as feelings of anxiety increased. Occasionally, I would lie in bed at night, staring outside at the campus, fearful that I might suddenly spring up out of bed and jump out of the window, freefalling to my death.

I stopped going to church on Sundays for much of the school year. I just could not find a reason to attend. I did, however, become much more involved on campus. In addition to a full course load, I started working at the South Quad cafeteria a couple times a week, and I joined several student organizations.

Even though my religious convictions were uncertain, my passion for social justice had remained intact. I became a writer for the Michigan Journal of International Affairs, the only student-run publication of its kind on campus, and wrote about Africa-related issues. I also joined a group called Children of Abraham (now United 2 Heal), an interfaith humanitarian organization that collected surplus medical supplies from local hospitals and distributed them to areas of need around the world.

Finally, I signed up for Dance Marathon, a campaign to raise hundreds of thousands of dollars for a children's hospital. This campaign culminated in a grueling 30-hour "marathon" during which all "dancers" were required to at least remain standing for the duration of the event.

It was at the Dance Marathon that I met a young man whom I will call Kris, one of the kids for whom we were raising financial support. I believe he was in middle school at the time, and we connected while playing basketball during the event. Kris had a spectacular jump shot, and I was really impressed.

Part of the reason he was so skilled, I found out later, was that he struggled with obsessive-compulsive disorder (OCD). Apparently, he would shoot the ball over and over again until his shot was perfect. At the time, I did not yet fully realize that I was beginning to struggle intensely with the same diabolical disorder.

I first learned about OCD in my freshman psychology class at U-M. Our textbook, *Psychology: Fifth Edition* by Peter Gray, said that "an *obsession* is a disturbing thought that intrudes repeatedly on a person's consciousness even though the person recognizes it as irrational. A *compulsion* is a repetitive action that is usually performed in response to an obsession. . . . People who are diagnosed with *obsessive-compulsive disorder* are those for whom such thoughts and actions are severe, prolonged, and disruptive of normal life." OCD was classified under anxiety disorders, or "those in which fear or anxiety is the most prominent symptom."

I remember watching a video in class about mental disorders. In the video, one man in particular had developed OCD during his early twenties, and eventually, the disorder become so severe that surgeons had to operate on his brain. I still remember the image of a large saw-like instrument hovering over him, ready to cut his head open. I began to fear that something like that could happen to me.

Even though symptoms of this disorder were manifesting themselves in ever-increasing intensity during my sophomore year, I had not yet fully recognized or admitted them. Mental disorders were for "weird" people, so I couldn't possibly have anything that severe; that just wasn't me, I thought. I suppose it was that very fear of the stigma associated with mental disorders, or perhaps my incredulity regarding the possibility that I could suffer from such a disorder, that caused me to wait so long before reaching out for help in significant ways. It wasn't until much later that I discovered the necessity of a solid support system and the beauty and freedom to be found in honest transparency with those who loved me.

CHAPTER
6

WAWA
(West Africa Wins Again)

It was the middle of the night, and we were some 37,000 feet above the dark waters of the Atlantic Ocean. Only a few dim lights were turned on, and the plane was quiet. I looked through my window at the clouds below. Suddenly, there was a flash of light, then another one. Lightning was striking from one cloud to another in tangled webs. The darkness below was illuminated by a full-blown electrical storm.

I sat there staring in awestruck wonder. Never in my life had I seen a storm like this from the sky. Instead of looking up at the lightning, I was looking *down* at it. A battle was raging below us, and we were soaring above the storm—a poetic (and perhaps prophetic) moment, to say the least. After several minutes, all was calm again, and I tried to fall asleep as best I could for the remainder of the flight.

After nearly eleven hours in the air, the airplane door finally opened. I felt the thick, humid West African heat fill the cabin. I grabbed my backpack, climbed down the steps on the side of the plane, and placed my feet on African soil for the first time. For many years, I had wanted to travel to the continent, and the moment had finally arrived. My three United 2 Heal teammates and I had come to Ghana to help secure the delivery of a 40-foot container of donated medical supplies and equipment to the Tamale Teaching Hospital, and our month-long journey in the country had just begun.

As soon as I exited the airport in Accra, I got hustled. I was pushing a cart with my luggage on it when a young guy walked up to me and said, "Welcome. It's your first time." He offered to push my cart for me, and because I thought he was an airport employee, I said, "Sure, thanks!" He showed me the "Ghanaian handshake", and I showed him what we do in the United States. He pushed the cart maybe 50 feet over to a taxi by the side of the road and then asked for $20 USD. I had not even requested a taxi. Realizing what was happening, I refused to pay him. A few moments later, I was approached by a woman begging for money, and again, I refused. I wanted to help, but I also thought that by giving to beggars, perhaps I would be contributing to a system designed to perpetuate poverty. I was an obruni ("white foreigner"), and for many people, that meant dollar signs.

Our guide finally arrived, and we drove to the University of Ghana, where we stayed for the first few days of our trip. The sights, sounds, and smells on the streets of Accra were both exciting and altogether foreign. Women in colorful, patterned dresses carried large baskets on their heads, and many had their babies strapped to their backs. Young children sold a myriad of products to drivers stuck in traffic, and large vans called "tro tros" packed with passengers made their way through the bustling city.

Businesses had names such as "God is Great (G.i.G) Sandals" and "Christ's Supermarket." When we arrived at the International Student Hostel on campus, I was glad that I had brought toilet paper because the bathroom had none.

Overall, my time in Ghana was characterized by both incredible, "once-in-a-lifetime" experiences and intense psychological stress and anxiety. (In my first journal entry from the trip, I prayed to God that obsessive-compulsive behaviors would not hinder my time in the country; but for whatever reason, I continued to struggle.)

At the beginning of the trip, we visited an organization that worked with physically and mentally handicapped people. I remember seeing a woman in her forties who was no bigger than a child. She had disfigured limbs, and she was strapped to a wheelchair. I'm not sure if she could speak or not. The image was burned into my memory, and it challenged me. This woman, although almost unrecognizable, was a human being just like I was.

A few days later, I attended Pastor Mensa Otabil's ministry in Accra, International Central Gospel Church (ICGC). Hundreds, perhaps thousands, of people filled the sanctuary, and it felt good to be in church again. After the service, we visited one of the biggest and most notorious slums in the capital city, known by some as "Sodom and Gomorrah." The level of poverty and destitution was surreal. A woman stirred a smoky, black cooking pot, and men in tattered clothing stared at us as we passed by. Walking through the winding maze of closely-packed tin shacks, I remember thinking, "How does one even begin to address this?"

I felt overwhelmed by the enormity of the problem and walked through in a daze, not even sure what I was feeling. Later that day, we attended an energetic soccer match in a large stadium, and that night, I discussed Ghanaian male-female interactions with a new friend of mine at a nice outdoor restaurant. Experiences were coming faster than I could process them.

Before our real work began, our team traveled to Cape Coast to visit two infamous slave castles that were a major part of the Trans-Atlantic Slave Trade. Inside Elmina Castle, a Portuguese church sat right across from a small, dark room with a skull and crossbones engraved above it: a prison with almost no ventilation in which, if my understanding is correct, unruly slaves were packed together and held until they died. Further along, the Door of No Return was the last sight that slaves saw before they were shoved onto the ships bound for the West.

The next day, we traveled to Kumasi, where we stayed with a host family for about a week. In the evening, we were invited to the host family's relative's house down the street—the place was a mansion. I could hardly believe my eyes: big flat screen TVs, contemporary décor, a beautiful courtyard, and balcony. We drank Sprites and watched a movie together.

On the drive back, we passed by small, tin shacks where other families were also passing their evening. The stark contrast between rich and poor troubled me.

Our days were spent volunteering at the Komfe Anokye Teaching Hospital (KATH), the largest hospital in the city. On one occasion, we were invited into a room where newborns were kept in baby bassinets. They were so tiny and fragile. Unfortunately, there were not enough bassinets, and one of the infants was simply placed on a desk in the corner of the room.

There were only supposed to be six bassinets in the room, but due to limited space at the hospital, the staff would pack in as many as thirty. One of the babies had an enormous, swollen head due to a blockage. Another baby's intestines were coming out. At lunch, I stared at my chicken and jollof rice, unable to shake the images.

My mental struggles made it difficult for me to focus throughout the trip, and as much as I tried to hide this from my teammates, they began to notice. As the four of us were playing Euchre one night, one of the young women said, "You don't notice much." The other chimed in, "You daze yourself out for whole portions of conversations when you're not actively involved." They were right; I found it incredibly difficult to concentrate or engage with the logistics of the trip. At times, my teammates would get frustrated because I could not seem to remember what was going on. My mind was clouded, and the world around me was often a foggy blur.

Near the end of our time in Kumasi, a pastor who was also a medical doctor at KATH shared his heart with us: "I could have twenty patients at the beginning of the week and ten patients by the end of the week. We live with an unseen expiration date. In my post-mortem work, I hold a man's brain in my hand. This is what he used in order to communicate with me yesterday—is this all there is to life? I have to keep a balance between doctoring and pastoring; I have a stethoscope in one hand and the Word of God in the other. It can be stressful work, but when you see people come alive, it's worth it."

We left Kumasi, and made our way north to Tamale on a bus.

Along the way, we stopped in a small town to use the restroom. We asked a woman where we could go to relieve ourselves, and she led us to an open area filled with vast heaps of garbage and filth. Goats and chickens picked their way through the rubbish. She couldn't be serious. About 50 yards off, some of the village children were lined up against a wall, staring at us. We had no other option. The girls turned one way and squatted, hiding themselves with their skirts, and the guys turned the other way.

At the next stop, Kintampo, I saw a poor, blind man begging for money. He looked like he had walked right out of a Bible story. I gave him what change I had, but I knew that he needed a lot more than what I was giving him. He needed a Healer.

We finally arrived at Tamale, and after waiting four long hours for our guide to pick us up, we made our way to Klass One Court, the small hotel where we stayed the night. The next day, the other young man on our team and I were introduced to our gracious homestay hosts: a 24-year-old medical student, and his older brother, a 28-year-old businessman (the girls stayed with another family). Our hosts lived in small, government-provided housing. There was a living room, a small kitchen, and a couple of bedrooms. The electricity usually worked, but there was no running water.

The two weeks in Tamale were perhaps the worst for me in terms of struggling with obsessive-compulsive disorder during the trip. I had intense, tormenting fears of contamination, and this led to obsessive cleaning. In the mornings, we had to shower using a bucket. I would take the bucket to another large container, fill up the bucket, and take it back with me to the concrete shower stall connected to the house.

Then, I would dump some of the bucket over my head to get my body wet, rub soap over my body, and dump the rest of the water to rinse myself off.

That would be challenging enough for most Americans, but it was even more difficult for me. The fears of contamination caused me to spend lengthy amounts of time attempting to scrub and clean every square inch of my body. At one point, I ran out of soap and had to use shampoo instead.

We had to wash our clothing by hand, using soap and water in a big washing bowl. I scrubbed and scrubbed my clothing, trying to get any contaminating elements out of them. The soap was drying out my skin, but I kept rubbing my knuckles against each other with the clothing in between to make sure everything was clean.

By the end, my skin was starting to come off my fingers. I tried to make the process look as normal as possible, but I imagine that others may have wondered why it took me so long to perform these relatively simple tasks. Back inside the house, I used hand sanitizer over and over again, until the smell seemed to fill the room.

During the days, our team worked with the staff at the Tamale Teaching Hospital to negotiate the arrival of the 40-foot container of medical supplies and equipment from the United States. It was a long, frustrating battle with an apparently inefficient bureaucracy. The hospital had previously agreed to pay the shipping costs for the container, but miscommunications slowed the process down to a snail's pace.

It was here in Tamale that we learned the meaning of "wawa." We were eating at SWAD, a restaurant that served American-style food (or as close as one could get in Ghana) when a white gentleman approached our table to greet us. He was from New York, but he looked like he was from Texas. He had a white mustache, a cowboy hat, and a Jesus belt buckle.

We learned in the conversation that he had lived in Ghana for the past seventeen years. He taught us that the term "wawa" was short for "West Africa wins again," a somewhat fatalistic sentiment which referred to the seemingly inevitable setbacks and inefficiencies that our group knew all too well by that point. "Always bring water and a book," he said. Good advice—we had learned that if one thing was for sure, there would be a lot of waiting around.

Interestingly, much of the hospital was open to the air. Patients lined the sides of the hallways, and a goat walked casually through the lobby area. We also spent time at Hands of Mercy Orphanage, where we brought gifts and played with the children.

The director had quit his regular job because God had led him to take care of orphans. There were seventeen kids, including three of his own, ranging in age from two months to fourteen years. With limited resources, he could only take in so many children at one time.

On the weekends, we took recreational trips outside of the city. We often traveled with another group from the University of Michigan that was also in the country at the time. Amazingly enough, one of the members of this other group was a friend of mine from Harvest Mission Community Church back in Ann Arbor. Having her there was a godsend. We had not coordinated our trips to coincide with one another's; it was only by God's providence that, even on the other side of the planet, I had a friend from back home.

We didn't know each other terribly well, but still, it was comforting to see a familiar face from my church on campus. On our way to the Crocodile Pond in Paga, we read together from a book entitled *Searching for God Knows What* and listened to worship music—it was a barely detectable ray of light in an otherwise confounded mind.

Once we reached Paga, each of us took turns sitting on a living, wild crocodile. A man would feed the crocodile a chicken, and we would sneak up behind the crocodile one at a time and slowly sit down on its back. It was incredible, realizing that this thing was breathing and that it could snap back at me at any time.

Back in Tamale that night, I called home for what I believe was the first time during my stay in Ghana. Even though I had only been in the country for a couple weeks, I felt deeply homesick, and it was a blessing to talk to my family again. I talked about some of my struggles with my Mom, and she told me that she had received a prophetic word from a pastor a few days earlier that she had never even talked to before.

He was prophesying about her children, and he said, "The one you've been concerned about, I'm taking the concern away. He's mine!" In that moment, I felt like God had not forgotten about me.

Whenever I could find internet cafes in the city, I would email my family. In one email to my parents, I shared feelings of guilt, hopelessness, and despair. I was frustrated with the logistics of getting the container of medical supplies to its intended destination, but I also felt a tidal wave of other emotions and struggles welling up inside of me. My Mom responded with this:

> All is well. I really think you can stop thinking so hard and just live.

I don't see how you can call your trip a failure. God knew the container would get stuck at the port before you ever left here, so easy does it, guy. And whatever else you feel you should be accomplishing, and aren't, could very well be your preconceived notions or expectations of what it would be like. Sometimes (no, almost ALWAYS) God's plans and objectives are very different from ours. We can think we aren't doing anything, or even "failing" at something and He is right on schedule with his hidden agenda. There are so many things He is accomplishing that we are totally unaware of many times.

I really see this trip as a seed—just a beginning—it's one thing to read (and study) about different people groups and cultures and nations, and it's totally different to go there and live among them for awhile. There is a certain level of exposure that the Lord is giving you.

It may not be a LIGHTNING BOLT experience but it may be what He wants for now, in this season, for His own reasons. None of us know exactly what your destiny looks like, but it will unfold as you go...(I've even heard Bishop Bismark say things like he really didn't think he was doing all that he was supposed to be doing...that he had not really come to his "destiny" yet.) So... It's God's job to lead, guide, protect and provide. We just have to trust and obey.

Please relax and enjoy the rest of your trip...you are a good brother, a wonderful son and an extraordinary person. You have much to give and you DO give. We all could be better (you don't know how many times I have felt like I have never really been the mother I need to be – and still am not – but I can't let it get me down or keep me from moving forward.) We are on this journey and we just need to trust the Lord to keep leading us.

We've got you in prayer, and as you know, you are on God's mind!! :)

Love you so much buddy,
Mom

During the last week of the trip, I became terribly sick. I was volunteering at the hospital and was literally on the verge of collapse. I went back to our homestay with a high fever, and the medical student we were living with said that he thought I had malaria. He gave me medication for both the fever and the malaria. Late at night, I tried to take the fever pills, but ended up vomiting all over the table and the floor. I went to the hospital for a blood test the next day, then took a taxi to Klass One Court, the hotel where we had spent our first night in Tamale.

I am forever grateful for the staff of Klass One Court. When they saw that I was sick, one of the managers brought me a platter with toast and hot chocolate, another staff member made me some fruit, and the man at the front desk played "I am the Lord that healeth thee..." over the hotel speakers. I had been feeling so sick, both mentally and physically, and the love that they demonstrated to me in that moment was incredible.

After a few days, I felt better, and although I was still struggling psychologically, the remainder of the trip was filled with beautiful moments and unforgettable images: a sunset from a hilltop overlooking the vast, green Mole National Park; wild antelope and elephants; a pitch black night in a rural village, looking up at billions of stars; a canoe trip down a slow-moving river; mud huts and tribal chiefs; a motorcycle ride at night through the streets of Tamale.

During our twelve-hour bus ride back to Accra, we stopped once again at Kintampo. I paid a small fee to use a restroom, and I was given a piece of newspaper—what could this be for? Upon entering the stall, I found out. I squatted down over a muddy hole in the ground, took care of business, and wiped myself with ripped pieces of newspaper. There was barely enough of the Spider-Man comic to do the job. My shorts now had a small amount of either mud or feces on them; I couldn't tell. I saw the same blind man that I had seen before, and once again, I gave him all the change I had.

I came back from the trip sunburned, mentally exhausted, and thirteen pounds lighter—skeletal, considering I was already underweight before I left the States. I felt like I had gone through some kind of trauma, and it took me awhile to recover. A few weeks later, a woman from the church asked, "Are you okay? You've seemed depressed since you got back from Africa."

Another friend said that I had come back looking like a concentration camp survivor—that was hyperbolic, of course, but not too far from how I felt at the time. The trip was another step toward a painful admission: I was struggling intensely with obsessive-compulsive disorder.

CHAPTER
7

Fear Hath Torment (In Over My Head)

"You know you're a hick when you come to your family reunion to pick up chicks." That was the joke circulating the Grenier Family Reunion that summer. "Grenier" was my maternal Grandma's maiden name, and the occasion drew dozens of relatives from across the country that I had never even met before. We had a great time laughing, reminiscing, and enjoying one another's company. I realized that there was something special about being a part of a large family.

It was at the Grenier Family Reunion that I met one of my cousins for the first time. We were all together at a BBQ in the neighborhood park, and every few minutes, I noticed that she got up to go to the restroom. She looked slightly dazed, and I found out that she had grappled for many years with OCD.

Paranoid of casually contracting HIV/AIDS, she would have to leave the room if she so much as saw an individual wearing a red "awareness" wristband. At the park, she was likely getting up every few minutes to wash her hands. In her late thirties at the time, she was also struggling heavily with alcoholism. A few months after the reunion, she took a leave of absence from her job and moved back in with her parents to recover.

In many ways, when I saw her, I saw myself. I saw the very thing that I was battling, and that was challenging for me. It was almost like looking into a mirror. I could identify with her struggle, and I began to wonder, "Could I end up enslaved by fear? Unable to move forward?"

Since that summer, my cousin has taken some tremendous steps forward. She is in recovery for both OCD and alcoholism, attends AA regularly, and works with a sponsor. In a recent email, she said, "My life is light-years away from where it was at the time of the reunion." Thanks be to God! My prayer is that she would continue to experience complete deliverance through the power of God's love.

That same summer, as I sat in the living room one night, I admitted to my Mom that I, too, was struggling with symptoms of obsessive-compulsive disorder. She had actually noticed some irrational and repetitive behaviors that had made her wonder. I don't remember what else she said that night, but I'm sure that she encouraged me and confirmed her love. It felt good just to get the truth out in the open.

For the rest of the summer, I napped almost every day. It seemed as if I could only find "peace" when I was unconscious, so sleep became an escape mechanism. Every day, my mind would become tormented, and eventually, I would collapse under the pressure.

*****

Sitting in the Fishbowl, a large computer room on the U-M campus, I was desperately attempting to piece together an essay for my History of U.S. Foreign Affairs course. The paper was due the next day, and I had just started. That was pressure enough, but on top of that, my junior year had witnessed only the increasing intensity of obsessive-compulsive thinking and behavior.

I sat there, staring at the screen. I would type a sentence, then delete it, then retype it. In a moment of inspiration, I would write a brilliantly composed thought; then I would delete it, thinking it was somehow "wrong" to use the words I was using. I replaced those words with synonyms, ever so slightly changing the meaning until the original thought was no longer recognizable. My mental faculties and powers of rational thinking were beginning to disintegrate—there were holes everywhere. My mind looked like Swiss cheese, and so did my paper.

When my GSI (graduate student instructor) returned the paper, I flipped to the last page to view my grade: C+. I was shocked. Never in my life had I received a grade that low on a paper. I got A's; that was just who I was. In fact, the last time I had received a B+ for a final grade in a class was 7th grade science, and to this day, I am convinced that the B+ was a computer error. I got a 4.0 in high school, and I had pulled A's for my entire college career thus far.

In my paper's bibliography, I had cited an article from Wikipedia because I had used it (among other sources) to gain a general overview of U.S.-Taiwan relations and thought it right to include it as a source—probably not the smartest idea. The GSI wrote something like this on the paper: "There have got to be better, more reliable sources on U.S.-Taiwan relations than Wikipedia. Please see me after class." I felt like going up to the GSI and saying, "Listen, bub, you obviously don't know who I am. I don't get C+'s." It was probably good that I didn't say that.

Eventually, I pulled a B+ in the class by busting my butt on a solid A final paper; it was my first B+ since that "computer glitch" in 7th grade science. I was frustrated not so much because of the grade itself; I was frustrated because I knew I could do better, but psychological torment was getting the better of me. Obsessive-compulsive thinking was beginning to significantly hinder basic functioning in everyday life.

One might suppose that someone with OCD would have an incredibly neat, clean, organized room. Not so, for me at least. The more paranoid and irrational my thinking became, the more disorganized and chaotic my world became. My environment reflected my mental state. Thus, my bedroom in my apartment was a mess. Things that I had thrown on the ground at the beginning of the school year remained there until the end of the school year. Everything was everywhere in the clutter and confusion.

As the Secretary of United 2 Heal, I struggled to take meeting minutes in the same way that I had struggled to write that history paper. Serving as a Regional Editor for the Michigan Journal of International Affairs—same story. I was barely limping along, trying to hold things together, but everything was coming apart at the seams. The weight of guilt and the torment of fear became familiar companions.

My classes didn't help. I took courses related to topics such as history, social justice, and African studies, and at one point, I think we were discussing genocide in nearly all of my classes at once. The human capacity for sick, deranged brutality caused me to become heavier still, and I feared my own potential for abuse and violence.

That year, I came to church more consistently, and I was more open with my accountability partner. Nevertheless, I was still spiraling downward, and it would get much worse before it got better.

*****

Washington, DC—summer 2010. My passion for social justice led me to accept an internship offer with the ONE Campaign, a self-proclaimed "hard-headed movement of people around the world fighting the absurdity of extreme poverty." The organization was co-founded by Bono (lead singer of U2) and now has over 3 million members and 60 million petition signers in 187 countries. As a Global Policy intern, I researched and reported on various international development initiatives. In my free time, I read books like *The End of Poverty* by Jeffrey Sachs, *Mountains Beyond Mountains* by Tracy Kidder, and *Banker to the Poor* by Muhammad Yunus.

I lived in a northeast townhouse near Union Station. A friend of a friend from church allowed me to rent out a small, second floor bedroom for $400 per month. Her bedroom was down the hall, and her daughter lived in the basement. During my first week, I explored the city on foot, seeing all that I could see—monuments, landmarks, museums—and at the beginning of week two, I made my way to 1400 Eye Street and began my work at the ONE Campaign.

As I often noticed in other places, DC was home to some tremendous disparities. On the one hand, the city was the seat of our nation's government, and it boasted a massive amount of power: the White House, Congress, the Supreme Court, the World Bank, international diplomats, embassies, K Street lobbyists, and the like. On the other hand, DC had some of the worst schools in the nation, and its streets were filled with the poor and the plighted—"princes" and "paupers" all in one town.

Every day, on my way to work, I walked by what was probably a blend of homeless beggars and hustlers. Some seemed mentally stable; others, not so much. I can still see one man sitting on a park bench, his head bent down so low that his chin touched his chest. The way his neck was hunched, he looked like he had been fixated in that position for years. Another man walked around the Metro (subway) terminal, yelling and cursing in a raspy voice that sounded demonically possessed. With just a tinge of irony, I got up each morning and went to work to "fight poverty."

I still remember sitting and reading on a park bench one summer day when a white van that read "Martha's Table" pulled up. Seemingly out of nowhere, about thirty homeless people gathered around the van. A container of water was set up, and the people lined up to fill their containers. As one man filled his bottle, another from the middle of the line called out:

"Don't take all of it. Leave some for the rest of us!"

"Mind your own business. I'm not going to empty this thing."

"You've already got half of it."

"I've got kids."

"I didn't need to know that. I did *not* need to know that! We all got problems."

That day, I purchased an issue of "Street Sense," a newspaper about homelessness, from a man on the corner. I learned from my studies about extreme global poverty that approximately 1.4 billion people in the world existed on less than $1.25 per day. I wanted to be a part of the solution; I wanted to help end extreme poverty in our world. I attended talks, went to conferences, and visited the offices of Members of Congress. I wrote these lines in my journal that summer:

> Another day, another dollar,
> I don't place my faith in dead presidents,
> Nor do I base my justice on unjust precedents,
> Pleading my case for the bottom billion,
> You might say I'm one in a million,
> But I wish there were a billion just like me,
> Screaming and dreaming for the end of poverty.

By the end of the summer, however, what came to characterize my time in DC was not passion for social justice, but mental anguish and torment. In many ways, this was the breaking point for me. In my small, second floor bedroom, with my belongings scattered all over the floor and my mind spinning like some kind of dark circus, I realized that I was truly "in over my head." The battle was bigger than me, and I could no longer fight it alone.

At work, I struggled just to type on the computer. Write, delete, write, delete. I tried to mask it as best I could. There was no spark in my eyes and very little life in my spirit. Almost 100% of my energy was focused on just trying to make it through the day.

So many days, as I walked to the Metro in the morning, all I wanted to do was collapse on the side of the road and wait for someone to find me. Surely someone who loved me would eventually find out what happened and come to rescue me. I just could not bear it any longer. Collapsing on the street, just giving up, was the most tempting thing I could think of.

Walking home from Union Station one evening, a man looked at me and said, "Hey man, Jesus loves you. Jesus loves you." The next day, I visited a church in Gaithersburg, Maryland, with a good friend of mine who lived in the area. After service, one of the church staff members looked at my t-shirt and asked, "What's ONE?" I explained to him that it was an anti-poverty organization. He responded, "I think you're pretty poor without Jesus. What do you think?"

A few days later, Bishop Smith and a group of young people from our church arrived in Washington, DC, on a trip designed to facilitate new cultural experiences for the youth. Connecting with my church family from back home was a ray of light and a touch of comfort in an otherwise cold and empty reality. We toured the White House and visited the Lincoln Memorial together. As our group boarded the bus, Bishop Smith asked me to pray, and I led a prayer for our nation.

The next day, I was scheduled to be in New York City. In addition to interning at the ONE Campaign, I was also interning online for the Zimbabwe Education Fund, and I had to attend a staff meeting in Manhattan. I left work early and found my way to the Bolt Bus stop, where there was a small crowd of people waiting for the bus to arrive.

As I stood there waiting, I was plagued by an intense, tormenting fear that I was going to abuse one of the other people waiting in line. The bus arrived, and I was still battling with this irrational fear. I almost didn't make it on the bus. In the end, I pushed through the fear, got on the bus, and took a seat.

The weight of guilt that descended on me in that moment was almost indescribable. "I shouldn't have done that," I thought. "I shouldn't have gotten on the bus. I shouldn't even be here." That thought consumed much of the two days that I was in New York.

The entire time that I was in the city, I kept thinking, "I shouldn't be here. If I had done things right, I wouldn't have gotten on the bus, and I wouldn't even be here right now." I felt as if my entire trip to New York was illegitimate, as if I was walking and living in some kind of alternate reality. I feared that none of those experiences should have happened.

However, one unforgettable moment from that New York trip will remain with me forever. I was walking through the underground maze of subways; all I could see and feel was the dirt, grime, filth, and slime. The environment felt grungy, and so did I.

As I made my way toward the steps that emerged to the light of day, I heard the melody of what sounded like a wooden flute sailing down the corridors: "Holy...Holy...Are you Lord God Almighty...Worthy is the Lamb, Worthy is the Lamb...." The beauty of that music just about stopped me in my tracks; it slipped effortlessly into my spirit and resonated in my soul.

I felt like breaking down and crying right there. I was remembering a feeling that had been too foreign for too long; I suppose I was remembering what it felt like to love and be loved by God, to simply let go and believe. Looking back years later, that one prophetic moment of "exiting the maze" could be seen as a metaphor for my entire journey.

But I was not out of the woods yet. I arrived back in DC, and the rest of my summer descended into madness. My small bedroom in the upper corner of the townhouse became a chaotic mess as I desperately attempted to avoid "contamination" from various items. The floor was speckled with loose change, pieces of candy, and small bits of paper. I had to sit in the corner and strategize how to get across the room without touching anything that was potentially "harmful."

In my mind, I was constantly at the mercy of a tormenting labyrinth of contaminants. I went through bottle after bottle of hand soap. Every time I touched something that was "contaminated," it meant another trip to the bathroom to wash my hands. Washing my hands was a complicated process on its own. I not only washed my hands, I washed the bottle of hand soap, the faucet handles, and then my hands again. To this day, the ink in my journal from that summer is smeared from the water on my hands.

Negative mental associations dominated my thinking, making daily tasks nearly impossible. For example, putting the cap on a tube of toothpaste came to be associated with ending someone's life, and because I could not break the seemingly arbitrary mental connection between those two ideas, I found it extremely difficult to complete the task. (For the next year or so, I always left the toothpaste slightly ajar.)

In particularly dark moments of fear and mental torment, I became completely paralyzed. Holed up in my room, I was chained in a mental prison that I could not escape. Perhaps the worst spell of paralysis took place on the first floor of the townhouse. I don't think anyone else was in the house at the time.

Fear was closing in around me like a boa constrictor, and I could not move. I twitched and jerked in small furtive movements, but I could not seem to go anywhere. For perhaps hours, I stayed in one spot between the dining room and the living room, locked in a stronghold.

First I was standing, then sitting, and all the while, I wanted to scream at the top of my lungs, but I could not scream. I wanted to cry out in anguish, but I could not cry. All was quiet on the outside, but my soul was being brutally and mercilessly tortured. I don't remember how I finally escaped; I probably came near to collapsing from pure mental and physical exhaustion.

On one particular rainy day, I approached the Metro station to make my way back to the townhouse. As I swiped my card at the kiosk, I seemed to notice that there may have been a small crack on the plastic covering for the sensor. Almost immediately, I began to fear that my card might have been wet from the rain.

"Perhaps some water got into the sensor through the crack in the plastic. Water mixed with electricity could cause an electric shock. That means that the next person who swipes in is probably going to get electrocuted. I should go back right now and fix it. If I keep walking, someone is going to be in terrible pain, and it's going to be all my fault."

Guilt pounded in my head, and my heart beat faster. I kept walking. I looked back, but kept walking. Standing in the Metro car, I watched the doors close in front of me. Guilt was throbbing through my entire being. The further I got from the scene, the heavier and more tormented I became.

Somehow, I made it up to my room, and after suffering for a while, I finally managed to call my Mom. She tried to calm me down as best as she could, but I felt guilty even about calling her in the first place. "I should be going back right now," I thought. Bishop Smith also called and tried to comfort me. Eventually, the noise in my head quieted down.

I almost didn't make it home that summer. Sitting in my room and looking around at my belongings, I could not fathom how I was going to pack my bags. There was too much contamination, and my mind was too fractured. My trains of thought kept slipping off the tracks and careening into the lake.

Just physically getting all of my things back into my suitcases was the most daunting task that I had ever been confronted with. It was like asking a quadriplegic to climb Mount Everest. Given the amount of psychological disorder I was contending with, I could not imagine how it was ever going to happen. My flight back to Michigan would be departing in a few days, but I was stuck.

I called my parents and told them what I was struggling with. I told them I could not seem to pack my bags, and I didn't know how I was going to make it home. My Dad's voice came through on the other end:

"Do you need us to come get you?"

"No, that doesn't even make any sense. You're going to spend all of that money and come get me just because I can't pack my bags? That's so ridiculous."

"Look, you are the most important thing right now. Making sure you're okay is more important to us than the money. We'll do whatever we have to do to get you home. Just say the word, and I'll hop on a plane and be right there."

Tears come to my eyes just thinking about that moment. The fact that someone would care about me enough to come and rescue me like that meant the world. I felt like someone loved me. I told my parents I would try to make it on my own if I could. I mustered what strength I had left, put my things together over several grueling days, limped my way to the plane, and by God's grace, finally made it home.

I learned one important lesson that summer: I could not fight this battle on my own. The struggle had gone beyond my powers of reason. I was in over my head, and I desperately needed help. I was humbled and broken.

CHAPTER
8

Confessions

The look on my younger brother Brian's face was one of shock and discomfort. Sitting across from him in his apartment bedroom, I had just explained to him what I had been struggling with. Although I had been fighting this condition for years, I had never revealed it to my brother. In fact, at that point in time, I could probably count on one hand the number of people I had talked to about it. Overall, the process of recognizing and admitting the problem, then overcoming the perceived social stigma of having a "mental disorder," was a slow one for me, but I needed to be open and tell the truth.

I tried explaining to him that I was still the same guy, that I just had not shared this part of my journey with him before, but he was still a bit stunned: "I'm just trying to process this...my brother has a psychological disorder." He was slightly freaked out, but he bounced back quickly. Brian was an irreplaceable part of my recovery process. He encouraged me, forced me to open up, and always infused a whole lot of laughter, fun, and spontaneity into the environment. Things were always better when Brian was around.

The beginning of my senior year was a whole series of "confessions," actually. During a special service at HMCC, I finally told Jesse, my roommate and one of my best friends. Chinese American pastor Jaeson Ma was the speaker that night, and he encouraged us to confess our struggles to each other. I felt the presence of God in that service. I was standing next to Jesse, so it seemed like an opportune moment to share my battle with him. I also told my LIFEgroup leader at some point during the first semester of that year.

Just the fact that some of my friends now knew what I was going through brought a small level of comfort. However, despite my baby step toward transparency, my senior year was perhaps the most difficult year of all, in terms of mental torment. It was also the most life-changing. The level of fear and confusion was almost unbearable, but I also began to experience some major breakthroughs.

Mental preoccupations seemed to come in "themes": a particular fear would spread like a cancer through my thinking for months (and even years) at a time. One of these tormenting themes was the fear of sharp objects: knives, keys, and even writing utensils.

On a more fundamental level, it was really a fear of self. I was afraid of what I perceived to be my capacity for sadistic violence, rage, and destruction. In my own head, I was a monster. I was scared that I might "snap" at any time, go out-of-my-mind crazy, grab a knife, and stick it into someone else. At any moment, I could lose control and commit some diabolical, deleterious act.

That fear confined me. For a long time, I could not even go into the kitchen of my apartment because there were knives in there. I would walk around it or come just far enough to grab something out of the refrigerator as fast as possible and get out. I remember going out to buy a slice of pizza from one of the dining halls simply because I could not enter my own kitchen to get food.

This fear eventually transferred itself to objects of a less lethal nature. I walked around terrified of the keys in my pocket. If my hands approached my pocket for some reason, fear struck my heart and my hands began to tremble.

I cannot tell you how many hours of my life I spent just trying to complete the most simple, mundane, daily tasks. For example, this scenario happened all the time: my phone was running out of battery. Any normal person would just hook the phone up to the charger and plug the charger in the wall.

For me, it was not that simple. For hours, I stared at the charger, trying to plug it into the electrical socket, but I could not do it. The mental association between plugging in the charger and stabbing/raping/abusing someone was too strong. The thought was so tormenting that I sat there crying, frustrated that I could not perform so simple a task.

Plugging in the phone charger became a moral issue. Sometimes, I would force myself to push through everything and just plug it in, and almost immediately, the guilt of having done so would force me to pull it back out again.

Another major fear, one that is apparently common among people who struggle with OCD, was the fear of leaving the oven on. I would check to make sure the oven was off. Then I would check again. Unconvinced, I would check again. And again. And again. Countless times I would go back to look again, not satisfied with the previous time.

I would think, "What if I didn't see it correctly? What if I accidentally hit it on the way out? I probably couldn't see things clearly. My mind is so confused, so how can I trust what I think I saw?" After checking and re-checking, I would somehow manage to break free and escape the apartment to go to class, but all day long, it was all I could think about.

"What if I left the stove on? The stove is probably on right now. Something is going to catch on fire, and then the whole house will go up in flames. If my roommates are inside, they could die in the flames. The whole building could come down, and I would be solely responsible. I would be the one to blame. It's all my fault."

Struggling with fear at that level, I did not even believe what my eyes saw. My eyes would tell me that the stove was off, but my mind would never be convinced. "I'm probably not seeing things correctly. I'm lost in a psychological maze. I can't tell what's real and what's not. How far away am I from the stove right now? I don't know. I have no idea. I can't tell."

I had questioned God my freshman year because I wanted to see to believe. Now, I could see what was right in front of me, but I still could not believe. The spirit of doubt and skepticism had taken over, and it was joy-riding through the playground of my mind.

As I brushed my teeth at night, sometimes my gums would bleed slightly. I thought, "Somewhere in the Bible, it says something against drinking blood, right? I shouldn't swallow my saliva right now because

I could ingest some blood along with it." So I would spit in the sink to try to get the blood out; but maybe I didn't get it all out, so I would spit again. Lying in my bed at night, I would continue to push the saliva out of my mouth. I kept a folded piece of paper towel with me in bed, and after it became completely soaked with saliva, I turned to my t-shirt and my bedsheets and continued to spit the "blood" out. Lying there, drenched in my own saliva, I thought, "This will be the last time. I won't do it again after this." Then, I would spit out the "blood" just "one more" time.

CHAPTER
9

Walking on Water

On September 14-15, 2010, Bishop Tudor Bismark convened the Detroit Regional Summit, a special two-day gathering for ministry leaders in the Greater Metro Detroit area. I attended the first evening session with my Mom and Dad. Prior to this, I believe my parents had mentioned my struggle with OCD to Bishop Bismark and his wife, Pastor ChiChi.

I don't remember exactly how it happened, but Bishop Bismark approached me unexpectedly to pray for me or something, and I just collapsed into his arms. He embraced me, and I just cried. All of the pain and confusion of the last few years was being released. My tears were dripping down onto his suit jacket, but he didn't mind.

Bishop Bismark was Bishop Smith's spiritual covering and the leader of the Jabula International Network. He had preached all over the world, and hundreds of churches were under his oversight. But more importantly to me, he was one of my role models. He was an inspiration to me. His words, his presence, and his care meant the world.

He spoke to me in a calm, comforting voice: "You're so brilliant. You will bring order to many things. That is your life—bringing order to confusion—and you're living some of that right now."

I came back the next evening, and before he graced the platform, he looked at me and said, "I've been praying for you." Near the end of the service, he spoke prophetically over me once again: "Destiny is never about the destination; it's about the journey. Some people who can see far into the future get frustrated with where they are. Don't do that. Enjoy being twenty-one. I never wish I was twenty-one again because I was a good twenty-one-year-old. I command order." Just days later, I wrote in my journal an idea for a book that I would write someday: it would be about my journey from confusion to order.

The emotional release comforted me for a moment, but my mind was still tangled in complicated webs of fragmented thought, and I continued to struggle. I could barely turn the pages of my reading assignments for school. I had to fight to get into bed at night. I even had difficulty speaking: just like that history essay back in junior year, I couldn't use the words I wanted to use. I spent much of the Christmas break vegetating, napping on the couch almost all day, every day, unable to do much else.

My Mom drove me back to school after break for my final semester at the University of Michigan. Before we arrived on campus, however, we stopped by Dexter, Michigan. I was scheduled to have a personal meeting with Bishop Smith. I remember sitting across from him in a small living room area next to his dining room table. He said something like this:

"Nathan, it seems as if you are, in some sense, lying on the ground, waiting for something to happen, waiting for deliverance to just come from somewhere. Instead, I hear God saying to you today, 'Rise, take up your bed, and walk.'"

My first thought was, "You really don't get it. You really don't understand where I am right now. I don't even know how to do that. I don't even know where to begin." But the seed of Bishop Smith's thought was planted.

He continued, "Healing doesn't usually just fall out of the sky. Healing comes from God, but it is something that you have to enter into. It's a dimension. Healing is like an ocean—it is always there; it is always available. But the onus is on you to dive in." I went back to campus not totally convinced but, thanks to Bishop Smith, with a new thought germinating in my mind.

Sundown on Saturday, January 15, 2011 marked the beginning of HMCC's two-week-long One Desire Fast. The first week, those fasting would eat only fruits and vegetables; the second week, only liquids. The purpose? To seek God with everything and to desire Him alone. I had participated in this fast the previous year but had treated it more like an opportunity to prove my religious piety, or to get God to prove Himself to me. This year was different. God had worked a measure of genuine humility in me over the past year, and I was ready to seek Him. No pretenses or pretensions—I just wanted to know Him.

He met me during that time. On the first Sunday of the One Desire Fast, I approached Pastor Seth after the Sunday Celebration to ask for prayer. He began to pray: "God, we know Your perfect love casts out all fear...."

That afternoon, I caught a ride back to my parents' house in Troy for a couple days. After struggling for a long time to complete a homework assignment, I ended up having a lengthy, late-night conversation with my Mom. We talked about finding the root issues of the obsessive-compulsive behavior, and we began to call to remembrance some of my childhood. My pride, my lack of submission, my strained relationship with my Dad, my feelings of rejection from a relationship in high school...it all played a part.

In that conversation, my Mom shared with me something that God had revealed to her: "This 'disorder' that you are struggling with is not primarily a chemical or physiological issue. At its root, it is a spiritual and emotional issue." Presumably, then, if I were to experience spiritual and emotional healing, then these other symptoms would eventually disappear. I went back to school and picked up my Bible for the first time in a while.

In His mercy, God opened up His Word to me in a revelatory way. Specifically, He began to minister to my spirit through the story of Peter walking on the water to go to Jesus (Matthew 14:22-33). Because this story became such a cornerstone of my recovery, I would like to include the passage here:

22 And straightway Jesus constrained his disciples to get into a ship, and to go before him unto the other side, while he sent the multitudes away.

23 And when he had sent the multitudes away, he went up into a mountain apart to pray: and when the evening was come, he

was there alone.

24 But the ship was now in the midst of the sea, tossed with waves: for the wind was contrary.

25 And in the fourth watch of the night Jesus went unto them, walking on the sea.

26 And when the disciples saw him walking on the sea, they were troubled, saying, It is a spirit; and they cried out for fear.

27 But straightway Jesus spake unto them, saying, Be of good cheer; it is I; be not afraid.

28 And Peter answered him and said, Lord, if it be thou, bid me come unto thee on the water.

29 And he said, Come. And when Peter was come down out of the ship, he walked on the water, to go to Jesus.

30 But when he saw the wind boisterous, he was afraid; and beginning to sink, he cried, saying, Lord, save me.

31 And immediately Jesus stretched forth his hand, and caught him, and said unto him, O thou of little faith, wherefore didst thou doubt?

32 And when they were come into the ship, the wind ceased.

33 Then they that were in the ship came and worshipped him, saying, Of a truth thou art the Son of God.

As God opened up my eyes to understand the Scriptures, the lights turned on in a series of personal revelations. The applications to my journey were obvious:

1. **When the disciples first saw Jesus, they were afraid.**

Although the disciples had spent time with Jesus, they were so consumed by their anxiety and fear in that moment that they were unable to correctly identify him. They became fearful of the only One who could possibly save them from their situation.

2.   **Peter recognized that his security was found in Jesus.**

He realized that he was safer trying to walk on water to go to Jesus than he was staying in the boat. He chose to forsake the ropes and the sails (his physical attempts to bring security) and decided to step out in faith. The safest place to be was with Christ.

3. **As long as Peter kept his eyes on Jesus, he could walk on water.**

When Peter stayed focused on Christ, he soared above all physical circumstances and achieved the impossible. When he looked back toward his situation, he began to sink.

4.   **When Peter cried out, Jesus reached out to save him.**

In the middle of a faith crisis, in the midst of fear, Jesus reached down to pull him out of the water, saving his life. When he stepped out in faith in response to

Christ's invitation, his safety was secured.

5. **It was the fourth watch of the night (the last watch before the dawn).**

At the time, I was in my fourth year of college and my fourth year of dealing with major doubts about God. I could not help thinking that perhaps this was not just a coincidence. The night is always darkest before the dawn.

This story became a very real part of my everyday experience. The waves of fear and confusion were constantly crashing around me, and I had been trying to cling onto the boat for dear life. But Jesus was out there, walking on the water, and I had to walk to Him. I began to take small steps of faith; when torment reared its head, I began trying to walk on top of it—to let go and trust God. As I continued to step out on faith, I slowly started to push the boundaries of what I thought was possible. The song "Storm" by Lifehouse illustrates the scene perfectly:

How long have I been in this storm?
So overwhelmed by the ocean's shapeless form
Water's getting harder to tread
With these waves crashing over my head

If I could just see you
Everything would be all right

If I'd see you
This darkness would turn to light

And I will walk on water
And you will catch me if I fall
And I will get lost into your eyes
I know everything will be alright
I know everything is alright

I know you didn't bring me out here to drown
So why am I ten feet under and upside down?
Barely surviving has become my purpose
Because I'm so used to living underneath the surface

If I could just see you
Everything would be all right
If I'd see you
This darkness would turn to light

And I will walk on water
And you will catch me if I fall
And I will get lost into your eyes
And I know everything will be alright

And I will walk on water
And you will catch me if I fall
And I will get lost into your eyes

I know everything will be alright
I know everything is alright

Everything's alright
Yeah, everything's alright

God also spoke to me in other ways during the fast. One morning, he put a Bible verse about rejoicing on my heart; then my Mom called and told me she thought I needed to rejoice that day. On another morning, He put Proverbs 3:5-6 on my heart: "Trust in the Lord with all thine heart; and lean not unto thine own understanding. In all thy ways acknowledge him, and he shall direct thy paths."

I said to God, "I think this is You talking to me; could You possibly just confirm it somehow throughout the day?" That day, I read an email from a friend, and as I scrolled down to the bottom of the email, this exact verse was a part of his signature.

Furthermore, I was at a church event that night, and a different friend of mine was closing out in prayer. He ended the prayer with Proverbs 3:5-6. You could make an argument that it was just coincidence, that Christians often quote this verse, but it just seemed a bit too coincidental to me.

On the last day of the fast, I attended HMCC's Friday night service for undergraduates. Pastor Seth spoke about surrender, about allowing God to take the pen and write the story of our lives. During the "response time" at the end of the service, he invited the church to come to the altar and place something there that symbolized our surrender to God.

I stood at my seat, struggling internally. I saw myself sinking in the water, like Peter. Jesus was reaching out His hand, but I could not take it. I sank deeper and deeper beneath the surface, looking up at Jesus' hand as it got further and further away. I wanted so badly to surrender, but in my mind, I could not.

For some reason, I felt as if I had come to church by the wrong path, that I had sinned in order to get here, and if I had done things according to the will of God, then I would not even be here in this moment. God quickly corrected me:

"Who do you think you are? If I say it is a good time to surrender, who are you to contradict me? Do you think you have to do everything perfectly in order to surrender?"

I couldn't come up with any worthy response. I cried out, "God, I just want to know for sure that you love me. Can you demonstrate your love in some tangible way?"

God seemed to reply, "Did you forget about the cross? I think I did that already."

After a few moments of struggle, I surrendered. I came up to the altar, kneeled down, and cried. I said, "God, whatever I can give up in this moment, I surrender." I took a pen from my pocket and placed it on the altar. For me, that pen represented three things:

1. My fear of sharp objects (and by extension, fear in general)
2. The journey of my life (and allowing God to write it)
3. The book that I would one day write about how God delivered me

As I went back to my seat, I felt freedom. I lifted my hands and worshipped in a way that I had not been able to worship in a very long time. The "high" of that moment only lasted a few hours, but the experience awakened something inside of me that could not stay suppressed for much longer.

CHAPTER
10

Untying the Knot

Although I was slowly becoming more transparent, most of my friends still did not know what was going on, and they often joked about my various eccentricities: how much soap I used when I showered, or how I always seemed to be taking a nap on the couch, or how seemingly "oblivious" I was to everything around me.

"Dude, how much soap do you use?"

"Typical Nathan—I come in, and he's crashed on the couch again."

"Well, Nathan wouldn't pick up on that. He's too oblivious."

Although it was irritating, I could not hold it against them. I had not been open enough to tell them what was happening, and they were just calling it like they saw it.

My last semester at U-M may have been the most difficult in terms of mental struggle. I only took ten credits instead of my usual sixteen or so, and that year, I had already dropped out of all of the student organizations that I was involved in. Due to my psychological state, I simply could not effectively manage my responsibilities anymore. This was the easiest course load that I had taken at U-M, but it was one of the most challenging to get through because daily tasks had become nigh insurmountable.

One of my African Studies classes was required in order to complete my academic minor, but not required for graduation, and during the semester, I considered dropping the course due to the intensity of my struggle. If I dropped it, I would lose the minor that I had worked so hard for during college, all because of OCD.

I was still working as a Food Service Worker in the South Quad cafeteria, but this only became another source of torment, and I dreaded going to work. As I served food to students who lined up during dinner, I became paranoid that while the plastic wrap that covered the serving trays was being removed, small pieces of plastic could have fallen into the food.

A couple of years prior to that point, I had spent time talking and laughing with other co-workers; now my mind was consumed with searching for small bits of plastic wrap that might possibly be in the food. As I served each student that went by, the fear and guilt became heavier. "There might be plastic wrap in the food that I just served them. They are walking away with their food right now, and I am not saying anything. I should say something. They could choke and die, and I could have prevented it. I am allowing people to die."

The paranoia was not limited to the plastic wrap. When I had to turn the burners off after a shift, I would check them multiple times, trying to make sure they were off. Almost invariably, I would walk away fearing that they were still on, and I thought that if they were still on, then perhaps something would catch on fire, and perhaps the entire building would go down in flames.

I had similar struggles with the pumps of cleaning fluid used to clean the surfaces of the dining hall. On one occasion, I left South Quad, walked across campus, and due to fearful debates in my mind, walked all the way back to make sure that I had shut things off correctly. I even asked a manager to help me make sure that everything was okay.

I left South Quad for the second time, and once again, due to intense mental anguish, I came back. Embarrassed, I asked the manager to answer a few more questions about the equipment. Obsessive, irrational fear was probably evident to him by that point.

Living on the U-M campus, I had no real need to drive a vehicle. Everyone walked or biked across campus, and my friends could drive if I ever had to go off campus. However, on one particular day during my senior year, I did have to drive.

I had not driven a car in a long time, and I was not mentally prepared for it. It took a lot of coaching from my Mom over the phone to convince me to get behind the wheel. I was almost physically shaking with fear. I thought that I might run someone over at any moment. I remember finally putting the car into drive, moving a few feet, then freaking out all over again, unable to go any further.

After more coaching, I hung up the phone again and drove for a few minutes, but anxiety was mounting and getting the better of me. Then, the car suddenly died, and I found myself parked in someone's driveway on a residential street. It was bitter cold outside, and it was getting dark. I waited for a long time in the freezing temperatures for

AAA to show up.

Eventually, I called my friend Jesse, and he came to pick me up. I climbed into the passenger seat of his car in desperate need of heat, and he had a tumbler of hot chocolate waiting for me. I had never been so cold. I sat in a daze, trying to recover both physically and psychologically.

*****

During my last semester at U-M, several members of the class of 2011 at Harvest Mission Community Church, a class we affectionately called Frontline, decided to participate in an Alternative Spring Break trip in southwest Detroit. We volunteered for a few days with Urban Neighborhood Initiatives, a nonprofit organization with a passion for making "urban neighborhoods vital, healthy environments that strengthen individuals and support families." We mapped out the locations of abandoned properties, catalogued various community art projects, and talked to high schoolers about the college experience. It was a fun and rewarding experience, and our team really bonded as a group.

On one evening back at the house we were staying in, someone decided that it would be a good idea for everyone to share his/her "life story." One by one, my friends began to share intimately and deeply about their journeys: their experiences, their pain, their struggles, and ultimately, the transformative love and hope that they had discovered in the redeeming work of Jesus Christ.

These were not short, guarded testimonies. Each person would share for perhaps 45 minutes, revealing extremely personal aspects of their lives. We did not get to everyone on the first night of sharing, so we decided to continue the following night.

I was not prepared to be that vulnerable, and I debated whether or not to share. Although I had been friends with these individuals for the past four years, I really did not want to be that open, and I hoped that perhaps we would run out of time before it was my turn.

I had not shared my struggle with OCD with most of the people in the room, and I feared that they would think of me differently after they heard about what I was going through. I was afraid that they might judge me, think I was crazy, or just be really weirded out. I really did not want people to think that I was strange, so I attempted to avoid sharing my story. During prayer one morning, however, I felt a strong conviction in my spirit to share openly and freely.

So I did. I told everyone about my family, my faith journey, and eventually, my ongoing battle with a psychological disorder. I put it all out there...and I was amazed by the response from my friends. Everyone in the room demonstrated so much love, acceptance, understanding, and support, and I was overwhelmed.

They invited me to come kneel down in the center of the circle, and everyone crowded around me, laid their hands me, and began to pray fervent, heart-felt prayers that God would bless me, keep me, and continue to transform my life by the power of his love. I began to cry. I could not believe that I had friends like this.

I had shared one of the deepest and most vulnerable parts of my life, and instead of judging or ostracizing me, they gathered around me to embrace me with nothing less than full and perfect acceptance. I felt the love of Christ in a very real and personal way, and I discovered what genuine friendship was all about—being able to share your deepest flaws and failures, and being loved anyway.

By the end of the trip, we had heard nearly everyone's life story (we finished some of them at "reunions" later on), and we were bonded together as friends like never before. We knew one another so much more intimately, and the atmosphere of love among us abounded. The willingness to be open and vulnerable, I had learned by experience, can create the potential for true and lasting friendships.

Everyone had a different story, but I found one unwavering truth in each of them: for one reason or another, everyone in the room needed the unconditional love of Jesus Christ. The love of God is the balm that heals all wounds, and love never ever fails.

*****

In late March 2011, I attended the annual Jabula Kingdom Conference. Presumably due to the intensity of my struggle and the level of confusion I was contending with, a personal meeting was set up between Bishop Smith, Bishop Bismark, and me. These two men of God were (and still are) spiritual giants, and I could hardly believe that I had been given this incredibly special privilege. I wished it were for some other reason, but it was an honor that I cherished nonetheless. We sat in Bishop Bismark's dimly lit hotel room, and he began to talk with me.

We covered a whole range of concepts in a short period of time, but this is one of his statements that impacted me most profoundly: "It's just organized chaos; even tangles are ordered." He went on to explain that every knot could be untangled. Under a magnifying glass, there were patterns even in the chaos.

The revelation of that thought was opened to me, and I realized that every tangled web of irrational thought in my mind could eventually be untied. God could straighten everything back out again. I saw all of the knots in my mind becoming clean, straight lines: entire networks of thought coming into realignment. I saw the knot of fear and the knot of guilt being unraveled. My thinking could really be straightened out. My mind could be healed!

CHAPTER
11

Grace to Finish

After a long journey through the dark, the lights were slowly beginning to flicker once again. I had discovered a great amount of truth over the span of a few months, but personal revelations notwithstanding, the daily mental battle still seemed relentless. The seeds of truth in my mind and in my heart had not fully matured yet, and in many ways, torment was still masquerading as my slave master, cracking the whip on a whim and forcing me to fearfully dart through twisted, black mazes and mental death chambers.

I still remember being completely paralyzed by fear—one day I "locked" myself in my apartment bedroom for about ten hours, unable to leave because I was so bound by fear. At some point, my roommate Jesse came in. He walked over to the top bunk and tried to gently talk me back to reality. Eventually, I was able to slowly come down from the bed. He talked with me and then led me to a birthday celebration that was being held for one of our mutual friends.

As I felt the jovial atmosphere of the party and heard the laughter of my friends, the intensity of the fear began to dissipate somewhat, and I began to come back to life. Most of the people at that particular party did not know about my struggle with OCD, and before Jesse left, he looked over at me to make sure that I would be alright. I nodded to confirm that I would. Once again, I had experienced true friendship. Not only did Jesse help coach me back to life in that moment, he also made sure that I was okay in a discreet way, covering my weakness.

I believe it was after this particular episode of "paralysis" that Jesse suggested that I seek out psychological help. I did not want anything to do with it. Jesse tried to explain to me that a psychologist was just a doctor for the mind. "If you were physically sick, you would go see a doctor, right? If you are having trouble psychologically, why not go talk to a counselor? It's the same thing. They are professionally trained to deal with this." Jesse even agreed to meet me after work and go with me.

I was still not entirely convinced, but I knew that I desperately needed help from somewhere. I told him to meet me after work, unless I called and said otherwise. At South Quad, right before I began my shift, I left a voicemail with my Mom letting her know that I was considering psychological help. She talked to my Dad and Bishop Smith and called me back before my shift was over.

The three of them recommended that I wait. They did not want to see me suffering, but they believed that there was another way—that we had not yet exhausted all of our resources. They had no idea what philosophies or recommendations the U-M psychologist would offer, and they wanted to amp up the prayer and the counseling from our end first.

At another point of intense struggle at home, my Dad, who could not stand to watch me suffer any longer, suggested the idea of medication. I refused. "No, I don't want to do that. I believe that God can deliver me from this condition. If He doesn't deliver me, then I won't be delivered."

Please understand that I am not saying that medication is a bad thing or that God cannot use tools like medication and secular psychological counseling to help restore a person. All I am saying is that for me, I felt convicted that God Himself was going to heal me without these other remedies—that He could perform the miraculous in my life. I did not want the glory to go anywhere else but to Him, and to this day, I can say that I have never visited a secular counselor and I have never taken any medication for this condition. God has truly worked a miracle.

As I neared the end of my final semester at U-M, I honestly could not see how I was going to graduate. I needed to write a 10-15 page paper for one of my classes and a 20 page paper for another class in order to pass. This may not seem like very much, but in my condition, it was the closest thing to impossible.

I could barely turn pages or type sentences. I had known about these papers for the entire semester, but due to my mental challenge, I had not even started writing them until less than two weeks before they were due. However, somewhere deep down, I believed that I would indeed graduate. Somehow, God would see me through this. Around this time, Bishop Smith made a pit stop on campus just to pray for me. I hopped into his car, and he prayed that God would grant me the "grace to finish."

My Mom had always been there for me when I needed her, but during this last semester of school, words fail to describe the sacrifice she made on my behalf. In the book of Hebrews, the writer mentions those "of whom the world was not worthy" (11:38)—those who had made such a significant contribution that they could not possibly be repaid.

During this time especially, my Mom was one in my life of whom I was not worthy—I could never repay her for what she did for me. She spent countless hours on the phone, trying to bring me back to life, back to reality. Because my mind was so broken, many of our conversations made no logical sense, but she continued to speak truth in love. She reminded me who I was in Christ, told me that I would one day have a powerful testimony, and affirmed her unconditional love. I know there were times when the burden of what I was experiencing became heavy on her, times when she wanted to just scream out of frustration, but she laid her life on the altar of sacrifice. God used the truth that she spoke and the love that she demonstrated to save my life, and I am forever grateful and honored to be called her son.

Around this time, the seniors at Harvest Mission Community Church were preparing for Grad Night, a special celebration at the church for all those who were graduating. During Grad Night, the younger classes would put together performances that highlighted the ways in which the senior class had blessed them, and the seniors would share brief, personal testimonies of God's grace during their college years. Each person's testimony had to be submitted ahead of time, so I began to type one. I put some thoughts together and emailed it to the person in charge. It was adequately personal, but nowhere near vulnerable. I certainly made no mention of any struggle with OCD.

As I thought about it more, I began to feel a conviction once again to be open with my story. It was now past the deadline, but I submitted a revised testimony, one that included the truth about my psychological struggle. Thankfully, it was accepted, and I was able to share it during Grad Night. As I stepped up to the platform, I looked out over the large audience (which included my Mom somewhere near the back), and I opened up my mouth to tell my story:

> I grew up with a strong Christian background. I was reciting the books of the Bible on TV when I was three years old, I went on two international mission trips, and was the president of my high school Christian club.
>
> When I came to college, however, I began to question everything about my faith. My doubts, questions, and uncertainties overwhelmed me to the point where I decided that I was not going to call myself a Christian any longer. I could not carry the label of a faith that I no longer firmly believed in.
>
> Along with this, for at least the past four years, I have struggled heavily with obsessive compulsive disorder. Basic daily tasks seemed nearly impossible. My thoughts would torment me, and I would be paralyzed for hours trying to work through psychological mazes. Many times, I wanted nothing more than to collapse and wait for someone to find me, someone to save me. I wanted to give up.
>
> But God rescued me. I reached a point of desperation and decided to reach out to God. And He responded. As recently

as this semester, He has revealed Himself to me, and He has shown me His power to heal and to save. As I surrendered to Him, He allowed me a freedom to worship, and in His presence, His peace loosed the shackles of my confusion. He was there for me, when I doubted Him, when I was angry at Him, when I refused to acknowledge Him. He has been working all along, and He loves me with an everlasting love. Though I am still struggling with this disorder, it is getting better, and I am believing God for complete healing.

God has used this ministry over the past four years to bless me, to challenge me, to comfort me, and to help bring me back to God. I do not have the words to thank those of you who have been such a blessing in my life, who have been there for me through all of my struggles. I love you all.

Thanks, and God bless.

What a relief it was to reveal the truth about my story, and in so doing, to glorify God. How freeing it was to be open with my struggles in an environment of love and support. Prior to this, I had heard that there was another student in the church who also struggled with OCD. I did not know who it was, but I thought that maybe my story would bless him or her in some way. It did not take long to find out. A brother from the church approached me during the after-party. "You were talking about your struggle with OCD," he said. "You know, I struggle with the same thing." Eventually, we scheduled a time to meet up over Thai food, and we talked together about our experiences and the hope that could be found in Christ.

But the semester was not yet over, and I still had two mammoth papers to write. In the last two weeks, I gave everything I had in me to finish those papers. On the last night before the due date, I stayed up nearly the entire night, fighting through mental torment and sleep deprivation, typing page after tedious page of meticulously-analyzed research. Somewhere around 7:30am the following morning, I completed my last paper.

Exhausted, I walked across campus to Ashley's a couple hours later, the bar where our class was meeting to chill with our professor and turn in our final papers. I handed my paper to the professor, and although I was physically and mentally drained, I knew when I left that bar that the semester was over.

I had done it. Or, more correctly, God's grace had carried me across the finish line. Not only did I keep my African Studies minor intact, I graduated summa cum laude with a cumulative GPA of 3.894. How great is our God!

On Graduation Day, I donned my cap and gown and walked into the Big House at U-M with an incredible group of friends to celebrate a remarkable achievement. My family was there to celebrate with me, as well as a homeless man I had befriended during the school year. After the ceremony, we walked out onto the football field and went outside the stadium to face the paparazzi—our loving friends and family.

We shouted and laughed and huddled together for group pictures. My family then took me out to eat at a nice Italian restaurant, gave me heartfelt cards, and announced that they were going to buy me a brand new suit to commemorate what God in His infinite grace had allowed me to accomplish. I never could have done it without Him.

CHAPTER
12

Houses of Healing

One of my favorite movies is *The Lord of the Rings: The Return of the King* (2003), directed by Peter Jackson. The film won eleven Academy Awards, tying *Ben-Hur* (1959) and *Titanic* (1997) for the most Oscars won by a single film. There are many reasons why I love this movie, and I will not list them all here, but one scene in particular from the extended version serves as a splendid visual for my experience during the summer after my college graduation.

Eowyn, one of the heroines, had been nearly destroyed by the powers of darkness while slaying the Witch-King of Angmar. Barely alive, she was taken to the Houses of Healing within Minas Tirith to recover from her wounds, both physical and spiritual. In the film, the Houses of Healing provided a calm, serene atmosphere of peace and wholeness, one that went far beyond mere medical treatment.

There was a spiritual component to her healing, and the entire environment was made conducive for holistic wellness and recovery: the soft natural colors, the soothing music, the gentle care. Through skilled healing over the course of time, Eowyn once again became conscious of the world around her and slowly recovered her strength. Eventually, she came back to life, both in body and soul.

After I graduated college, my family and I agreed that it would be good for me to take some time off before pursuing a career. The intensity of the mental struggle during college had taken its toll on me, and I needed some time to heal and recover. I moved back in with my parents and began to attend Embassy Covenant Church International more regularly. These were my Houses of Healing.

Many of my friends were busy securing jobs, moving to other states, and becoming financially independent, but I would not have traded this time with my family (and my church family) for the world. God used this time in my life to fill me with His healing, His rest, and His peace. I was being built up in my inner man, and God was laying the foundation of my future in my spirit. He was siphoning the poison, and filling me with His life and His joy deep down in my soul. He was allowing me the space and the time to breathe and receive rejuvenation. Looking back, I can think of no better place to be than where I was.

At the instruction of Bishop Bismark, I memorized Psalm 91, a reminder of God's constant and unwavering protection:

> **1** He that dwelleth in the secret place of the most High shall abide under the shadow of the Almighty.
> **2** I will say of the Lord, He is my refuge and my fortress: my God; in him will I trust.

3 Surely he shall deliver thee from the snare of the fowler, and from the noisome pestilence.

4 He shall cover thee with his feathers, and under his wings shalt thou trust: his truth shall be thy shield and buckler.

5 Thou shalt not be afraid for the terror by night; nor for the arrow that flieth by day;

6 Nor for the pestilence that walketh in darkness; nor for the destruction that wasteth at noonday.

7 A thousand shall fall at thy side, and ten thousand at thy right hand; but it shall not come nigh thee.

8 Only with thine eyes shalt thou behold and see the reward of the wicked.

9 Because thou hast made the Lord, which is my refuge, even the most High, thy habitation;

10 There shall no evil befall thee, neither shall any plague come nigh thy dwelling.

11 For he shall give his angels charge over thee, to keep thee in all thy ways.

12 They shall bear thee up in their hands, lest thou dash thy foot against a stone.

13 Thou shalt tread upon the lion and adder: the young lion and the dragon shalt thou trample under feet.

14 Because he hath set his love upon me, therefore will I deliver him: I will set him on high, because he hath known my name.

15 He shall call upon me, and I will answer him: I will be with him in trouble; I will deliver him, and honour him.

16 With long life will I satisfy him, and shew him my salvation.

In the early part of the summer, I joined Harvest for a Fopact (Focus + Impact) Retreat designed for graduate students and single working adults. Although half of my mind was consumed with thoughts of plastic wrap that could be in my family's food at home, I nonetheless felt an intense desperation for God.

I broke down crying in nearly every session of worship; all I wanted to do was be with God. If I was with Him, then everything would be okay. I was putting my faith into action in a very tangible way, applying what I learned from Peter walking over waves to go to Jesus. Moment by moment, I tried to push beyond fearful, irrational thoughts and attempt to touch God. It was difficult for me, but I hoped that if I went to God with every situation, then He could work everything out. During a morning devotional time, I flipped open my Bible and began reading. After a few verses, I realized which story I had landed on: Jesus was telling the paralyzed man to rise up and walk.

A little while after the retreat, I went to support Bishop Smith as he ministered to a church in Port Huron. I believe he spoke on the subject of "Divine Justice"—God would always balance the scales in a person's life. At the end of his message, he called me up to where he was standing and introduced me as a "son of justice."

He asked that I stand behind him, put my hands on him, and pray for him as he prayed for justice in the lives of the people in the church. It was a powerful moment of ministry, and I felt like, if God could use me like this, then maybe I really was where I was supposed to be. Maybe He really did love me.

Back at Embassy, Bishop Smith asked me if I would be willing to be the Co-Director of the church's Human Dignity Department, the branch of the ministry that was dedicated to engaging in humanitarian outreach and addressing societal issues around the world. Although I was in a time of rest, I was excited by the idea, and I was more than willing to serve in that capacity. I began to research the intersection between Christianity and social justice in the Bible. I scanned nearly the entire Bible, making a list of each passage that dealt with poverty, justice, and compassion. I wanted to make sure that we had a strong theological understanding of the Church's role in the arena of social justice as we attempted to address some of the issues in our society.

That June, I took a five-day trip to New York City to visit a brilliant friend of mine who had started a nonprofit to help children get a quality education in Zimbabwe. We had been friends for years, and I wanted to learn more about how she started her organization. She had also offered to introduce me to another friend of hers who was a graduate of the Harvard Kennedy School of Government, a school that I was considering applying to.

In addition to the meetings that I scheduled, I took the opportunity to tour the city. I experienced Times Square, Central Park, Ground Zero, the United Nations, Wall Street, Broadway, the Statue of Liberty, Ellis Island, and Brooklyn Tabernacle, all in a few days. This was nothing like my last stay in New York, in terms of mental anguish. I was still struggling with some things, but overall, there had already been a marked improvement in my mental clarity, and I was functioning on a more optimal level.

Near the end of the trip, I received an important call. Bishop Smith wanted me to share my testimony with Embassy that Sunday morning. I arrived in Detroit on Saturday night and began to collect my thoughts.

The following morning, I stood in front of my church, and once again, I opened up to tell my story. What a moment of joy—to honestly and publicly share this amazing journey with my church family.

I also had the opportunity to contribute to *The Vine*, a student-run publication for O@sis, the Chinese youth group I attended in high school. The editors of *The Vine* were releasing a special edition for Senior Sendoff, a night devoted to blessing the senior class as they transitioned to college. As before, I had an opportunity to share both my struggles and my ultimate victory over them through Christ Jesus. I did not mention my challenges with OCD on this particular occasion, thinking that it might be too much for my audience. (However, I later shared the full story in person at O@sis during another event.) I ended *The Vine* article with the following suggestions:

1. **Trust God no matter what** – God loves you with an everlasting love, and he will never leave you or forsake you. He's got your whole world in his hands. Bring every situation to him, and believe that he has the power to work things together for good.

2. **Join a Christian community** – God blessed me with Christian brothers and sisters in college who were there for me during my times of struggle. God will often use his Body (the church) to strengthen those who are weak. Fellowship with your Christian family can be a great way to experience the love of God.

3. **Live for something bigger** – Bigger than yourself. Bigger than your personal ambitions or career goals. This life is about God's love and glory. Allow him to use you as the salt and light in the world. Champion a cause. Join a club. Speak for the oppressed. Share the gospel of Jesus Christ. Show love to that person no one seems to care about. Surrender to God, and let him use you to bring change to the world.

On August 28, 2011, the Human Dignity department hosted its first major outreach: a volunteering event in southwest Detroit in partnership with Urban Neighborhood Initiatives (UNI). About 40 volunteers worked together to clear a pathway that children use to walk to school and clean up an illegal dumping site in a back alley. I was thrilled—Embassy members were out in the community, making a tangible difference. In a small way, the Church was really being the Church. Two months later, we held a screening of 58:, a film about the global Church's role in addressing extreme poverty around the world. The title comes from Isaiah 58, a chapter in the Bible in which God reveals His heart about justice and compassion.

Around this time, Bishop Smith began to teach a sermon series at Embassy entitled "Rest," a message that changed my life forever. (Eventually, I would assist Bishop Smith in writing his first book, *No Want, No Fear: Discovering Rest in Christ*, based on this series.)

Through this particular teaching, Bishop Smith showed believers how to escape needless stress and anxiety and find complete peace in

Christ. The basic premise was derived from Galatians 2:20, "I am crucified with Christ: nevertheless I live; yet not I, but Christ liveth in me: and the life which I now live in the flesh I live by the faith of the Son of God, who loved me, and gave himself for me."

If we are crucified with Christ, then we have no carnal wants and no fears. We are dead to our old nature. Then, when Christ resurrects Himself in us, we take on His nature, and we are filled with His grace to accomplish His will in the earth. We want only what He wants, and our only "fear" is a reverential respect for the only true and living God.

The "Rest" series fundamentally shifted my thinking, and I began to receive a sense of stillness and peace from God. I found that I could live a life free from carnal desires and irrational fears, and I could find deep and lasting rest and security in Jesus Christ. My old nature was dead, and the new nature of Christ was alive in me. While assisting with the book that Bishop Smith published based on this series, the message became even more solidified in my spirit.

Immediately after the "Rest" message, Bishop Smith followed up with a capstone series on the subject of "Pure Grace." Jesus Christ, in dying on the cross, satisfied the righteous demands of God's justice. He took the full brunt of God's wrath against sin, and He paid the full price of redemption for all of humanity in a beautiful exchange — the innocent for the guilty, the just for the unjust.

He died in our place, and His righteousness was imputed to us by the pure grace of God. As believers, all of our sins have been forgiven — past, present, and future. Although there can be earthly consequences for sin, no matter what mistakes we make, God has paid the price for every one of our failures, and He loves us fully and unconditionally. I can think of no greater reason to rejoice.

*****

At home, my family began to love me back to life. The warm atmosphere of peace and comfort slowly melted the irrational fear and anxiety. Many times, I would find myself in a familiar place of painful mental torment, screaming inaudible screams and searching restlessly for solutions to nonexistent problems. In those moments, reason did not always work; but love did.

My Dad would sit next to me and wrap his arms around me, and I would burst into tears, crying like a baby. All I really wanted was to be loved. I wanted someone to understand where I was and love me anyway. My Dad let me cry in his arms, and then he would bring me a plate of hot food, just trying to help me feel better. As I felt my father's love, the problems I was trying to work through in my mind became less and less important, and eventually, they dissipated.

I remember going through a particularly bad moment of struggle, sitting on the living room couch, explaining to my family that I felt like no one really loved me. I knew intellectually that they did, but I just could not feel it. My twelve-year-old brother Matthew, who couldn't bear to see me in that state, couldn't hold back any longer. "I love you!" he said. He was so genuine, and once again, that's all it took for me to break. He gave me a big hug, I cried again, and my heart was healed that much more.

The consistent, unwavering love that I experienced from my family played a major role in healing me from obsessive-compulsive disorder, and I am confident that the power of unconditional love can heal an entire host of mental disorders. I learned by experience that "there is no fear in love; but perfect love casteth out fear: because fear hath torment. He that feareth is not made perfect in love" (1 John 4:18). Love conquers all, and love never fails.

CHAPTER
13

Trust Me With Him

My parents played such an integral role in my journey that I would like to provide them with an opportunity to share part of it in their own words.

From my Mom, Mary Lou Cole:

So off to college he went. I could feel part of me going with him. It's not easy to let go—it's bittersweet, actually. Half of me was so excited for Nathan to take this next step toward the fulfillment of his destiny, and the other half was full of emotions as memories of the last 18 years flooded my mind.

I decided that I was going to be a "big girl" and wait for him to make the first contact. I refused to be a helicopter parent! Yes, I would give him his space, let him stretch his wings and meet new people, and allow him time for new experiences, as well as time to get settled and adjusted to his new environment.

Then one morning, there it was—an email in my inbox. I was more than excited! Quickly, however, my heart began to sink as I read about how he was questioning his faith. A rush of thoughts began to compete for expression in my head:

> *Surely this couldn't be true! Not our son! Not Nathan!*
> *His foundation was so solid!*
> *So much had been invested in him!*
> *He has so much promise!*
> *How dare the enemy!*

Any parent that has a relationship with the Lord wants His very best for their children. Apostle John said it so well: "I have no greater joy than to hear that my children walk in truth" (3 John 1:4). There truly is no greater joy for a parent than that. If their children are in relationship with the Lord and walking in the light, they will have everything they need to successfully complete their God-given purpose on earth.

But here I was, faced with the cold, harsh reality that somehow doubt had crept in and Nathan was unsure of his very foundation. No longer was he standing on the Rock; he was on shifting sand and had lost his assurance of security.

I finished reading his email knowing full well that Nathan was in a battle and that I had just been given major material for prayer. But before I even uttered the first prayer, the Lord spoke four words to me:

"Trust Me With Him." I had no way of knowing then how long, or to what depth, those words would have to carry me.

Thus began the journey of walking with Nathan to places and experiences that were totally foreign to me. It started with questions... endless questions...concerning the existence of God, the meaning of good and evil, etc. Nathan has always been an extremely intelligent and analytical thinker, so his questions were deep, complex, and thought-provoking.

I recall when he was only seven years old, he was asking questions and debating as a scholar would, and one of my best friends said to me, "Lou, I'm glad he's yours and not mine. I don't know what you're going to do with him!" What she meant, of course, was that she was unable to answer his questions...at only seven years old!

As time went on, the degree of irrationality, the mental confusion, the twisted logic, and the seeming absence of all reason and basic common sense was extremely difficult to even comprehend, let alone navigate!

The truth is that Nathan's faith was so deeply rooted in him that he couldn't see it. Every now and then, he would say something that would make me laugh because (little did he know) his faith had just made a surprise appearance.

One of the most challenging portions of the whole journey was the long conversations on the phone, most often late at night. Nathan suffered so badly—he was terribly tormented. He was afraid of hurting someone, afraid he left the burner on at work, afraid of somebody choking on a piece of plastic wrap that covered their food, afraid, afraid, afraid.

The fears were diverse, endless, and without foundation. And truly, fear has torment! With God's help, I tried to counsel, console, encourage, share the Word of God, reason with him (which very seldom worked), and pray for him.

Many times, he would ask me to pray and get an answer from God as to what he should do in that very moment. Most times, that would help him for the immediate situation, but it was very short lived.

It was excruciating to watch Nathan go through this and not be able to help him. When he was at his worst, it seemed nothing I did made any difference. He slipped to places where I couldn't reach him at all—not by talking, or praying, or any other means.

Certainly inherent in the heart of a mother is the desire to protect her child. (Ever see a mother bear with her cubs?) If the child is in danger, the mother will risk her own safety to rescue the child. All I wanted, from an emotional standpoint, was to see the pain and torment end. I just wanted Nathan to be able to feel better and thoroughly enjoy his college years. But from a spiritual standpoint, I knew that God was working on something much larger and deeper than I could see. He was digging an incredibly deep foundation that could support a superstructure!! I began to ponder, "Just who is this young man? I mean REALLY who is he, that he would go through such a fire as this?"

What kept me grounded in all of this was that I knew he was in God's hands. When no one else could reach him, God could, and that was exactly how God wanted it to be. Nathan was on a journey with his God. He needed his own testimony, his own "I know that I know" encounter with God. He was an adult now (albeit barely), and he couldn't borrow our experiences anymore. Yes, he had his journey, and by default, I had mine!

When Nathan was seven years old, I had a miscarriage. I absolutely dreaded telling him the news because of how badly he wanted the new baby. I toiled with it awhile, but eventually, my husband and I had to tell him. I braced myself for his reaction.

He cried, as expected, but within just a few hours, he said to me, "Mommy, I'm okay with it. No man took the baby. No demon took the baby. God took the baby, and He doesn't make any mistakes." I was amazed! It was a mature response for sure, but what blessed me more than that was the fact that God had already taken his little heart in His hands (the heart I was trying to protect) and helped him to process the whole thing! We MUST trust God with our sons and daughters. No one can do a better job with them than He can!

I cannot tell you how many times over the four years of Nathan's college experience that the words God had spoken to me came back to me: "Trust Me With Him!" Oh, the power of a Word from the Lord! Oh, the strength it brings, the faith it inspires! Without faith in God, I honestly don't know how I could have managed those difficult years. I had to lean on Him so heavily!

And let me say here that having faith in God doesn't mean that He won't use people in the process. Bishop Hugh D. Smith Jr., our pastor, spiritual covering, and friend, was greatly used by God on Nathan's journey. Bishop Smith had already been such a gift in our lives—and he still is, now more than ever. He is one of the most godly men I have ever met. Only God knows the hours of prayer and counsel that he invested in this one very special young man. It was as if Nathan was his own son.

I remember one day in particular that he had met with Nathan for several hours at his house. That evening, I told Bishop Smith some of the irrational things that Nathan was still saying and the level of challenge that he was still experiencing—just hours after their extensive meeting!

At that point, anyone else might have thrown up their hands and said, "I give up! I have given this my best and yet no change!" But not Bishop Smith. He deeply believes that God has a destiny and purpose written in the heavens for every person, and he dedicates his life to helping people manifest their God-given purpose.

Bishop said to me, "This thing is tearing me apart. I am going to fast until something breaks! You and Dave can join me if you want." What comfort this brought, to know that we were not in this alone. It is difficult to adequately express the gratitude we have for real covenant relationships. God never intended for His people to be isolated. We are His body, fitly joined together, and every connection, every joint, supplies something. There is so much that depends on relationships! So, thank you again and again, Bishop Smith!

Throughout this journey, I had to look at everything Nathan was experiencing through the eyes of faith. I couldn't allow myself to be swallowed up by my emotions when matriculating through this maze. I HAD to keep my eyes on the end and remember that "better is the end of a thing than the beginning thereof" (Ecclesiastes 7:8). I had to know (not just believe) that God loved him and that this was NOT how the story would end! I had to remind myself of his destiny, the contribution he was purposed to make to humanity, and the potential he had to change the world and make it better in some extremely significant way. I had to see the fruit of all this pain and keep my eyes on the prize. For the joy that was set before me, I had to endure this painful cross.

Several times I got weary, sometimes I grew impatient, and many times I cried, but the Lord's words were my anchor and my strength. I knew somehow, and at some point, the Lord would bring him out. After all, he had been bought with a price—he belonged to God! And he was not a victim! He was an overcomer! I refused the lies that the enemy wanted him (and, at times, me) to believe.

Sometimes, you have to command your mouth to speak life, to speak hope, to speak victory, to speak all those things that you know are true but are simply refusing to manifest in the moment.

At some point, it became obvious that Nathan responded to love and support. Even though he was tormented, he seemed to find some level of comfort from the love that was shown to him. Just knowing someone cared (and that they at least tried to understand) seemed to provide some level of security and stability.

One day, I asked God, "What are we dealing with? A mental disorder? A chemical imbalance?"

The Lord answered and said, "It is spiritual and emotional." There was an obvious correlation between how far Nathan had dropped in his faith in God (in God's very existence) and how far he had plunged emotionally and rationally.

Nathan was healed in phases, and I watched the Lord bring him to a place where he allowed himself to simply believe, whether or not he could empirically prove anything. At some point, the dark days became less intense, and the time between them grew longer. There were still challenges, for sure, but Nathan was able to come out of them more quickly. It was an indescribable joy to see Nathan smile again, and laugh, and have a bright light shining through his eyes. We had our son back, but after his journey with God, he was better than ever! He emerged with an unshakeable foundation, a commanding presence, and a passion for God (and for the things of God) that is truly inspiring. The hand of the Lord upon him had crafted a finer vessel, one now meet for the Master's use! I am eternally grateful to the Lord for His faithfulness, His love, His mercy, and His compassion!

From my Dad, David Cole:

Nathan started behaving somewhat abnormally to my adult understanding when he was a student in high school. Teenagers tend to sleep during growth spurts, take long showers till the hot water is gone, hang out late with friends, and sleep in late till someone wakes them at the inconvenient hour of eleven o'clock or through the smell of bacon permeating into their room. All of this is somewhat normal, but Nathan's behaviors were excessive.

As a father, I tried to coach him to structure his day by getting to bed earlier, not staying out so late, saying "no" to a few things, and allowing time for his mind to rest. I thought that having a pattern set for the day would help correct what I was observing, but it did not. In fact, the more I tried to provide constructive advice, the worse the behaviors manifested. This made no sense to me. I thought that Nathan was just "acting out" to get either attention or some other thing that might be lacking in his life.

No matter what I tried, Nathan became worse, to the point that one day when I was trying to correct him, he literally went into the fetal position at the end of the couch as if he was being beaten. It was then that I realized that he and I were both lost. Instead of trying to fix him, I just went over to him, held him, and told him that I loved him and that I would do whatever it would take to help him. We both broke in that moment. Just the small act of reconfirming one's love and commitment can cause tremendous healing. This small gesture did not seem relevant at the time, but it was really the solution.

Bishop Smith, our pastor, is very skilled at drilling down to the root of a matter. Nathan and I journeyed to his home one afternoon and were prepared to present ourselves "naked" (holding nothing back) to get to the truth of the matter. I was really prepared to take a beating since Nathan and I had previously had rough spots in our relationship that may have had an impact on him.

I didn't care about how I might be viewed or judged by others; I just wanted Nathan whole again. The torment I saw in him trying to rationalize a very basic situation was heart-wrenching. To anyone else, what he was attempting to rationalize would not have even been a topic of discussion, but to Nathan, trying to get on the bus or not could involve hours of mental argument. Therefore, getting to the root was very important.

The diagnosis hurt. I had missed the mark by not affirming and re-affirming my son. I had never had a lesson on being a father. I did not have a list of role models that dealt with the ideas of imparting and mentoring. My world was working hard, bringing home the paycheck, fixing things around the house, attending baseball games, running errands, mowing grass, taking out the garbage, and going to church. And start it all over again next week. Nathan was a part of my world, but he relied heavily on his mother for affirmation.

As a young man, I went through a period of rejection that had a damaging effect on my life. In order to cope with it, relationships were held at a distance. As long as I let no one get close to me, I could survive. Part of the rejection damage was the feeling that my opinion did not matter and my words had no weight. The silence of my words deprived my wife and sons of the father's strength.

Many people do not know the strength of their words or their value to others. A fit and timely word can set a course and inspire great perseverance. A father's word is designed to be generational. What a son receives from his father is meant to be passed down to the next generation as an inheritance. Being a father is a special privilege and also a place of responsibility.

After my experience as a young man, it was not until I married a person who truly loved me that this barrier I created to cope with rejection became difficult to maintain. Love was wearing it down, and I was becoming free. Over time, unconditional love released me to be a father and to finally see what I was designed to do.

I owed Nathan a lot of years of love and time.

By first fixing my issues, I was able to address Nathan's need through confirming my love to him and praying for his healing. The Nathan that was tormented is no longer; instead, I have a tremendous son with great talents and open doors waiting. I now look for opportunities to speak into his life and support his dreams and aspirations.

CHAPTER
14

Embracing the Journey

I looked out of my hotel room window at the Harare skyline and could hardly believe that I was in Zimbabwe. I had wanted to come to this country for so many years, and by God's grace, I was finally here! This was the home country of Bishop Tudor and Pastor ChiChi Bismark, two of my greatest inspirations. I remembered Bishop Bismark talking about Zimbabwe when I was in middle school, and the country had been in my heart and mind ever since.

My parents had been here in 2005, and now, seven years later, here I was. Before I left the States, one of my aunts had encouraged me over the phone: "You've got a lot of walking on water to do!" As far as I know, she had no idea how much the idea of "walking on water" meant to me; but God did, and I took it as a personal encouragement from Him.

My purpose for this trip was two-fold: to attend an annual Jabula Conference hosted by Bishop Bismark and to conduct a needs assessment for a Human Dignity medical initiative. I had traveled with Bishop Smith, and a few days later, we were joined by Human Dignity Co-Director Phallon Treece, who arrived from Italy. I was back in Africa, but this time, it was different. This time, I could feel the presence of God with me, and that made all the difference.

When the plane touched down in Harare, I was excited. A dream of mine for many years had finally been realized. Bishop Smith and I were briefly delayed by security guards at the airport, but our host arrived shortly and got us into the country. We were then taken to the five-star Meikles Hotel in the heart of Harare—per the arrangements made by Bishop Bismark's staff.

While in Zimbabwe, I saw unacceptable levels of poverty in slums like Mbare, but I also saw an industrious, entrepreneurial people committed to the ultimate success of their nation. Amidst extremely adverse conditions, there was an incredible faith that things were changing for the better—that the next ten years would not be the same as the previous ones.

The Jabula Conference was incredible. Perhaps 6,000 people were packed into the Rainbow Towers conference center, many of whom had been waiting outside for an hour and a half just to get decent seats. An award-winning choir from Bishop Bismark's ministry, New Life Covenant Church, sang in multiple languages: Shona, Ndebele, Zulu, English, etc. People found their way to the open dance floor at the front of the auditorium and worshipped God with a joy and enthusiasm often unseen in the States. Grammy Award-winning artist Israel Houghton led worship with New Breed, and leaders from around the world propelled us prophetically into the future.

As Israel, and the rest of the auditorium, sang, "Your love for me is overwhelming...," I opened up my heart to God and experienced something incredible—for a moment, I felt as if time had ceased to exist, as if I had stepped into eternity. A deep sense of peace and joy filled my spirit, and I took in the moment—I embraced where I was in that very moment. I felt the continuum of my life—past, present, and future—and I knew that I was exactly where I was supposed to be and that I would remember this moment forever. It was almost like an out-of-body experience; I was in the moment, conscious of myself experiencing the moment, and completely persuaded that this moment was a preordained, defining moment in the course and destiny of my life.

In that moment, God allowed me to experience a deep sense of trust and joy that for so long had been foreign to me. I felt complete and peaceful. It was as if I was living something that I had already lived before—I was simply remembering. God was actively changing me from the inside out, by the power of His overwhelming love. Tino tenda, Jesu!

*****

The manner in which I experience life today would not have been possible just a few years ago. The mental clarity, the emotional development, the spiritual consciousness—all of these were mere fantasy, but thanks to Jesus Christ, they have become a part of my reality.

God called me out of the darkness of psychological torment into His marvellous light, and my world has never been the same. I have experienced levels of peace in my personal prayer time that I did not think possible—peace that goes beyond understanding. Fear and anxiety are dissipating as I continue to discover what it means to love and be loved by God. What an incredible privilege to witness God's life-transforming power.

However, this transformation did not happen overnight. There were many powerful moments along the way (like the one described above), but there was no lightning bolt of instantaneous deliverance. It was a journey—and one that is still progressing. When Bishop Smith was counseling me through this journey, he reminded me that healing is often a process.

Even in the Scriptures, Jesus did not heal everyone immediately. Some were told to go show themselves to the priest and complete the purification rituals prescribed in the Law of Moses. These individuals were healed *along the way*, as they journeyed to their destination. On another occasion, a blind man first saw men as "trees walking" before he finally regained full visual clarity. In a more extreme example, Jesus actually waited until Lazarus *died* before arriving on the scene to demonstrate His power to resurrect the dead.

Although my healing did not happen in a single moment, I can say with undeniable certainty that God has transformed my life. There is a "night and day" difference between where I was just a few years ago and where I am today, almost as if God spun me around 180 degrees. I am not plagued by the level of torment that I previously experienced, and I am living life with a whole new sense of freedom. Thanks to the love of God, the irrational fear and confusion has been replaced by peace and trust.

My prayer for the year 2013 was for wholeness. I wanted to experience wholeness and completeness in every area of my life. I wanted to be one with God and one with myself. By the end of that same year, I had discovered the fact that manifested wholeness in a person's life is not really an event, per se. Wholeness, instead, is a place—a dimension in Christ. Wholeness is a state of being, one that can be accessed and experienced at any time by exercising faith in the sacrifice of Jesus Christ on the cross. My wholeness has already been purchased and needs only to be received by faith.

That said, every once in a while, that familiar enemy of fear will attempt to slip its way back into my thinking. It will knock at the door of my mind, just to see if I will answer. In those moments, I am compelled to pray, if for no other reason than to remind myself (and that enemy) who is in charge.

Even writing this book was a journey, at times fraught with anxious thoughts and fears, but when I commune with God, I remember that He has given me power over all of the power of the enemy. I remember that I am victorious in Christ Jesus, that I have won the victory through His sacrifice, and that I cannot be defeated. In prayer, I resume my rightful position of authority and refuse to be bound.

Sometimes, for me at least, prayer is more of a necessity than a choice. Bishop Smith once said to me that God wanted to "dance" with me and that if I just held onto His hand and flowed with Him, everything in my world would be filled with the peace of God. However, if I let go of His hand and fell out of sync with Him, things would begin to tumble around me.

Whenever I feel myself beginning to stumble, whenever I sense the static of chaos in my thinking, I know that I have gone too long without intimate communion with God, and I find myself on my knees again, seeking oneness with Him.

My desire is to be with God and to experience Him more fully. Here is a brief journal entry from February 7, 2012, that gives some expression to my heart's cry:

> I want to live in unprecedented peace, grace, love, joy, righteousness, etc. I want it to be beyond anything I've ever experienced. A whole new dimension of reality in Christ. I want to soar on wings as eagles (Isaiah 40:31). I want a merry heart and a continual feast (Proverbs 15:15). I want to feel like I'm flying by the grace of God. I want God's love and life and holiness to just explode inside of my spirit. I want to dance before the LORD with no inhibitions. I want to live without fear. Maybe then I can inspire others to live without fear as well. Pure and holy passion.

January 12, 2013:

> I want to receive a DEEP TRUST of God, something down in the depths of my soul. He is the Alpha and the Omega, the beginning and the end. All of time and all of space is in his hands. Every problem, issue, and quandary has already been accounted for, factored in, and worked out in Christ Jesus. God sees the intents and movements of the heart, and he is just, fair, and merciful. All things will be laid bare. All things shall be

brought to light. I believe him for his grace and his mercy.

God, I love you. You are the only one that matters to me. I want to know you better, to be closer to you. I want intimacy, Lord God. Father, friend, healer. You restore my soul. You give me a reason to keep living. You fulfill me in all of the deep places of my soul and spirit. You are the one for whom the depths of my being are longing. All I need is you. You are the Comforter. You are my peace and my joy. You are my love. Fill me to capacity, God. Let your love and your Spirit overflow to the world around me. Stretch me, God. Increase my capacity.

If ever I feel anxiety, I know that I am in need of a fuller understanding of who God is and who I am in Him. Fear is nothing more than a lack of revelation of the love of God, for we know that perfect love casts out all fear.

Just as light and darkness cannot occupy the same space, fear and love cannot coexist; love is the antithesis of fear, the antidote for anxiety. God is love, and there is no fear in Him. The more quality time I spend with God, the less I fear.

CHAPTER
15

The Defeated Foe

"It's not about hanging on. It's about letting go." That's what my friend said about indoor rock climbing, a hobby she had recently taken up. The fear of falling, she explained, would actually prevent one from being able to climb effectively. She was, of course, wearing a safety harness, and she said that she actually practiced falling several times just to overcome the fear associated with it. Once fear had been conquered, she was free to strategize the ascent and fully enjoy the experience. Another friend showed me an incredible YouTube video of infants who were swimming almost effortlessly on their backs. I could hardly believe my eyes—with some simple training, these babies were peacefully floating all by themselves. My friend looked at me and said, "Fear is a learned behavior."

As my journey unfolded, it became very apparent to me that fear was one of the major root causes of the psychological torment that I had experienced. While recovering from many of these mental struggles during the summer of 2011, I listened to a song called "Always" by Kristian Stanfill. One of the lines in the chorus says, "I will not fear." I thought the claim was somewhat strange. How could someone *choose* not to fear? Was that even possible? At some level, I thought that fear just "happened." Fear was something that I had no real control over. It came and tormented me at will, and I was a powerless victim who couldn't do anything about it. In my mind, that's just the way it was.

Slowly, however, God began to reveal the errors in my thinking, and he began to show me that fear is most certainly not an uncontrollable condition. On the contrary: fear is a choice. A powerful verse in Revelation illuminates this point in a subtle but potent way:

> But **the fearful**, and unbelieving, and the abominable, and murderers, and whoremongers, and sorcerers, and idolaters, and all liars, **shall have their part in the lake which burneth with fire and brimstone**: which is the second death. (Revelation 21:8, emphasis added).

The question that stuck out to me was the following: why are the "fearful" going to the lake of fire? How can a just God send someone to hell simply for being afraid? Now, we know that God is just, so the problem is not with Him. Therefore, this verse seems to indicate that human beings have the ability to choose whether or not to fear. That means that we are not victims; that means that we actually have authority over this sick, diabolical plague called "fear." As believers, we have the power to end its unlawful tyranny in our lives.

Let's examine this point from an even wider perspective. When humanity sinned against God in the Garden of Eden, God brought a curse upon all Creation. Thorns and thistles sprung up from the ground, men worked by the sweat of their brows, and women discovered pain in childbearing. Disease and death entered the world, and a once pristine paradise was lost. As God relentlessly pursued a renewed relationship with humanity, He eventually revealed His Law to Moses on Mount Sinai in the Old Testament. If the children of Israel, God's chosen people, lived according to the Law, then they would be blessed. However, if they disobeyed the Law, they would be cursed.

What I find incredible is that, for those who were under the Law, "peace" was a part of the blessing, and "fear" was a part of the curse. Leviticus 26:3, 6-8 states the following (emphasis added):

> If ye walk in my statutes, and keep my commandments, and do them;
> **. . . And I will give peace in the land, and ye shall lie down, and none shall make you afraid**: and I will rid evil beasts out of the land, neither shall the sword go through your land.
> And ye shall chase your enemies, and they shall fall before you by the sword.
> And five of you shall chase an hundred, and an hundred of you shall put ten thousand to flight: and your enemies shall fall before you by the sword.

The capacity to enjoy a fearless life was a part of the blessing for those who kept God's commandments. God actually gave peace as a gift to those who walked in His statutes. However, verses 14-17 and 36-37 reveal the flip side of the coin (pay particular attention to the sections of the passage I bolded):

> But if ye will not hearken unto me, and will not do all these commandments;
>
> And if ye shall despise my statutes, or if your soul abhor my judgments, so that ye will not do all my commandments, but that ye break my covenant:
>
> I also will do this unto you; **I will even appoint over you terror**, consumption, and the burning ague, that shall consume the eyes, and cause sorrow of heart: and ye shall sow your seed in vain, for your enemies shall eat it.
>
> And I will set my face against you, and ye shall be slain before your enemies: they that hate you shall reign over you; and **ye shall flee when none pursueth you.**
>
> . . . And upon them that are left alive of you **I will send a faintness into their hearts** in the lands of their enemies; and **the sound of a shaken leaf shall chase them; and they shall flee, as fleeing from a sword; and they shall fall when none pursueth. And they shall fall one upon another, as it were before a sword, when none pursueth:** and ye shall have no power to stand before your enemies.

When I read this description of fear in the Bible, I was astounded by how well it paralleled my own experiences with OCD. The passage describes an irrational, delusional fear that ultimately causes self-destruction. God appointed terror over His people, meaning that terror became their master. Fear ruled over them.

The people would flee when no one was chasing them, and the "sound of a shaken leaf" would cause them to run and fall upon each other. I knew that feeling quite well: infinitesimally miniscule details causing debilitating fear. Just like those under the curse in the passage, I had spent countless hours fleeing when no one was pursuing, putting out fires that had never even existed.

Even more astounding, however, is that every curse of the Law (including the curse of fear) was completely broken in Christ Jesus. When He died on the cross, He "became" sin for humanity and took every curse of God's judgment upon Himself. With His perfect sacrifice, He fulfilled the righteous demands of God's justice and paved the way for humanity to enter into renewed relationship with the Father.

The just was offered up for the unjust, the innocent for the guilty. He took our unrighteousness from us and imputed His righteousness to us. Every curse was broken. Thus, when we believe and receive the sacrifice of Christ, we can walk freely in the blessings that He purchased for us on the cross, including the peace mentioned earlier. Paul makes this point clear in his letter to the Galatians:

> Christ hath redeemed us from the curse of the law, being made a curse for us: for it is written, Cursed is every one that hangeth on a tree: That the blessing of Abraham might come on the Gentiles through Jesus Christ; that we might receive the promise of the Spirit through faith. (Galatians 3:13-14).

Fear was one of the major curses of the Law, and as we can clearly see from this passage, Christ has already redeemed us from all of those curses and allowed us to receive His blessings. That means that fear has already been vanquished. Fear is a defeated foe. Through faith in Jesus Christ, the power of fear has been broken. When we believe in the finished work of Jesus Christ, we are no longer subject to the torment of fear.

Furthermore, the blessing of God's peace has been released to us through the cross. The peace of God has been given to us freely as a gift. All we have to do is open up our spirits in faith and receive it. Jesus shares this truth with His disciples before He goes to the cross:

> Peace I leave with you, my peace I give unto you: not as the world giveth, give I unto you. Let not your heart be troubled, neither let it be afraid. (John 14:27).

Jesus is the Prince of Peace, and He has given His peace to us—what a life-changing thought. If we, in hunger and faith, open ourselves to Him, we can receive His peace. It really is that simple.

Fear is nothing more than a lack of love: a lack of genuine, consistent intimacy with Christ. Fear is a void. It fills the empty spaces that are created when love from the Father is not fully embraced and experienced. When we know in our hearts that we are loved fully by God, fear ceases to exist. Perfect love casts out all fear. That means that the antidote to needless anxiety in our lives is a quality relationship with Jesus Christ.

Incidentally, the admonishment to "fear not" in the Scriptures is often followed by a reminder that God is with us. The fact that God is with us is the greatest reason not to fear. This truth can be found in many places, including one of the most commonly quoted passages of Scripture in the Bible—Psalm 23.

In this familiar psalm, verse 4 says, "Yea, though I walk through the valley of the shadow of death, **I will fear no evil: for thou art with me;** thy rod and thy staff they comfort me" (emphasis added). The more conscious I become of God's presence with me, the less I fear anything else in my environment.

The first question God ever asked humanity in the Bible was "where are you?" Often referred to as the "first missionary call," this question revealed God's desire to be with humanity. In this particular case, God was reaching out to Adam, trying to renew a broken relationship with humanity after the Fall.

God was accustomed to communing with Adam in the Garden, but after Adam ate from the forbidden tree, this communion was no longer possible without divine intervention. Adam and Eve were exiled from the Garden of Eden, and God has been seeking to restore communion with humanity ever since. That, in fact, is the centerpiece of the entire Bible and indeed all of human history—God's relentless desire to be with us.

After the Fall of humanity, God made a series of covenants with the patriarchs of the Old Testament in attempts to bridge the gap. Leviticus 26:12 reveals God's intentions: "And I will walk among you, and will be your God, and ye shall be my people."

At the end of the day, God just wanted to be with His people again, to walk among them and commune with them. However, the carnal nature of mankind ultimately prevented them from living up to God's righteous standards, and God could not be with a sinful people. After all, "what fellowship hath righteousness with unrighteousness? and what communion hath light with darkness?" (2 Corinthians 6:14).

So God resorted to the only possible remedy—He sent His only begotten Son, Jesus Christ, into the world to restore a relationship with humanity by paying the price for sin. When Jesus appeared on the scene, He fulfilled an ancient prophecy:

> Now all this was done, that it might be fulfilled which was spoken of the Lord by the prophet, saying, Behold, a virgin shall be with child, and shall bring forth a son, and they shall call his name Emmanuel, which being interpreted is, **God with us.** (Matthew 1:22-23, emphasis added).

The Word was made flesh and walked among us. Jesus was the fullness of the Godhead bodily, and He gave up his life on the cross to reconcile humanity back to God.

He died for prostitutes and sinners, beggars and tax collectors, the nothings and the nobodies. He died for you, and He died for me.

Jesus sacrificed Himself so that we could have renewed relationship with the Father, and through Him, we can experience fellowship and communion with God forevermore. This communion is about cultivating a sense of intimacy and oneness with God. The Bible describes marriage in terms of two individuals becoming one:

> For this cause shall a man leave his father and mother, and

cleave to his wife; And they twain shall be one flesh: so then they are no more twain, but one flesh (Mark 10:7-8).

The Church is the Bride of Christ, and we were meant to be one with God. At the Last Supper with His disciples (often commemorated as "Communion"), Jesus offered up a prayer for His Church, a prayer for oneness:

Neither pray I for these alone, but for them also which shall believe on me through their word;

That they all may be one; as thou, Father, art in me, and I in thee, **that they also may be one in us**: that the world may believe that thou hast sent me.

And the glory which thou gavest me I have given them; **that they may be one, even as we are one:**

I in them, and thou in me, that they may be made perfect in one; and that the world may know that thou hast sent me, and hast loved them, as thou hast loved me.

Father, I will that they also, whom thou hast given me, **be with me where I am**; that they may behold my glory, which thou hast given me: for thou lovedst me before the foundation of the world.

O righteous Father, the world hath not known thee: but I have known thee, and these have known that thou hast sent me.

And I have declared unto them thy name, and will declare it: that the love wherewith thou hast loved me may be in them, and I in them (John 17:20-26, emphasis added).

As I was recovering from my challenges with OCD, my Mom encouraged me to take Communion every day, meditate on God's love, and let His love fill me. Just days after she spoke this to me, I met with Bishop Smith, who said that God had spoken to him about me that morning.

It was then that Bishop Smith told me that God wanted to dance with me. I would be spinning from His hand and flowing with Him in a harmonious kind of way, and I would begin to stumble if I let go of Him. He said that I needed to be in a state of "constant communion" with God and that I would learn what it meant to truly pray without ceasing.

I would be able to experience what Paul and others in the Scriptures were talking about. I could get "caught up" in God and go places in Him. I have an ability or tendency to lock in on one thought or idea, to become fixated on something. If I directed that toward God, I would remain in communion with Him and experience a level of intimacy with Him that our generation desperately needs.

As believers, God is not only with us for a moment; He is with us always. He has promised that He will never leave us nor forsake us, and we will be with Him for all of eternity, fellowshipping and communing with Him forever. His perfect love has already annihilated every conceivable fear, and we are free to fully enjoy the profound peace of His presence. My heart is full just thinking of it.

CHAPTER
16

Finding the Answer

When I first began struggling with my faith, I asked a seemingly endless number of questions about God and truth, often to no avail. For years, I lived without any answers that I deemed to be sufficient. No matter how well others would attempt to explain the "rationale" for God, I remained unconvinced; nothing could satisfy the doubt that I had allowed to creep into my soul. In some sense, I think that I was actually not looking for the answers with a sincere, honest heart. Instead, I was taking the position of a disbelieving skeptic and demanding that God prove Himself to me. He eventually did, but not in the way that I expected.

I do not believe that there is anything wrong with asking honest questions; I think God wants us to be curious—hungry for more knowledge and understanding. For example, God spoke to Moses from the burning bush only after He saw that Moses turned aside to see why the bush was not being consumed. Moses was seeking for understanding, and God revealed Himself in a powerful way. Jesus said, "Ask, and it shall be given you; seek, and ye shall find; knock, and it shall be opened unto you" (Matthew 7:7). He encourages us to pursue greater revelations of Him.

However, I do believe that the *manner* in which one asks a question can make all the difference in the world. My Mom likes to illustrate this particular point by contrasting Zacharias (the father of John the Baptist) with Mary (the mother of Jesus). Both of these individuals experienced angelic visitations, and both of them asked a question of the visiting angel; but they received vastly different responses.

When Zacharias asked Gabriel a question, Gabriel said, "And, behold, thou shalt be dumb, and not able to speak, until the day that these things shall be performed, because thou believest not my words, which shall be fulfilled in their season" (Luke 1:20). Later in the same chapter, when Mary asked a question, she received an answer that provided her with clarification.

Zacharias asked his question from a position of disbelief and doubt, and therefore, he received a sharp rebuke. Mary, on the other hand, had a believing heart and asked her question because she was honestly looking for greater understanding.

After all of the faith-related questions that I asked near the beginning of this book, one might naturally wonder, "Did you ever find the answers that you were looking for?" I would say, more than finding the "answers," I found *the* Answer. God may have answered some of my individual questions, but for the most part, He just *became* the Answer.

In other words, when I discovered God and began to seek Him

honestly for who He really was, I discovered that almost all of my previous questions became completely irrelevant. When I found myself in His presence, the arguments that I had made against Him were no longer important to me. They were trivial, frivolous, purposeless.

Instead of dissecting each question that I posed to Him, God chose instead to bring the entire conversation to a higher level. As the God of the universe, His very Being is the Answer to every question, quandary, and complexity. He supersedes all finite logic and reason and goes beyond all understanding to solve every enigma.

As one reads through the Gospels, one finds that Jesus answered people in a similarly profound way. Jesus would address the question that was on the heart of a person—not necessarily the one that came from their lips. That is what He did for me, as well.

He knew that deep down, I was not really looking for answers to all of the questions that I was asking. My constant questioning was only an outward manifestation of something much more fundamental: in my heart, I was hurting.

I felt rejected by God, abandoned by Him. I felt lost and confused, and I allowed my mind to rebel against God, even though my spirit—the spiritual core of my being—still believed in Him and wanted desperately to believe without constraint.

Somewhere deep inside of me, I never really stopped believing and loving God, as crazy as that may sound, given the way that I have described my story. I know this because even in the darkest days of my spiritual and psychological struggles, there were moments when my innermost spirit would connect with God.

I would often cry, speak in tongues, and remember briefly what it felt like to just allow myself to believe. My Mom often pointed out how comical it sounded to listen to me talk: I would form a "logical" argument against the existence of God and, almost in the same breath, would proceed to share something that I had recently prayed about. It was like I was talking out of two sides of my mouth. I was a double-minded man—unstable in all my ways—a house divided against itself that could not find a way to stand.

After a couple years of tiring, repetitive debates about the existence of God with one of my LIFEgroup (church small group) leaders during college, he finally said something like this: "Look, let's go beyond the question of God's existence and get to the real question. I think you actually do believe in God, but there is some deeper issue that you are grappling with that is causing you to deny His existence. So let's table that whole discussion about whether or not God exists. What is the real question, the real issue, you are dealing with right now?" As much as I hated to admit it, and as much as I wanted to continue spouting out my case against faith, he had pretty much hit the nail on the head.

Even though my spirit believed in God, I allowed my mind, my intellect, to take control of the rest of my being. My mind usurped authority over my spirit and attempted to lead the band, to my undeniable detriment. When my spirit would begin to experience God in an intimate way, my mind would soon step back into the frame and remind me how "irrational" all of this really was.

Under the tyranny of the flawed, unredeemed intellect, chaos ensued. It was only when I finally gave my spirit permission to resume its rightful place of rulership within my being that I began to enjoy peace and prosperity once again.

The mind is a useful tool, but it must not be allowed to take complete control, in terms of determining the direction and course of one's life. As one common saying so accurately states, "the mind is a wonderful servant but a terrible master."

Only the Spirit of God within an individual can truly discern that which is most valuable and precious in the sight of God, and it must be the guiding light that gives purpose and meaning to the vessels of the soul. One of my journal entries from mid-2012 gave voice to this newfound understanding:

> My spirit, and the Spirit of Christ within me, is a covering for my mind, my emotions, my imagination, etc. It covers, it guides, it shields, it blesses. If my mind tries to rise up and dominate my spirit, it will lead to sure and utter destruction.
>
> It is only when my reality is informed by the Spirit that everything else makes sense, that everything falls into place and finds its proper balance, when the world is at peace. My spirit can learn something and know something that may take my mind ten years to catch up with and fully understand and embrace. That is one good reason why the mind must not be in control. It is a subsidiary vessel.
>
> The spirit is limitless. The spirit can soar beyond the constraints of rationality and logic [into] a peace that passes all understanding. Peace that makes no sense because it transcends comprehension. It cannot be grasped. It is beyond and complete.
>
> The Spirit should inform the mind, inform the will, inform

the emotions, inform the imagination. It should fill up these vessels to capacity with its fullness and propel them forward farther than they could ever have gone on their own.

Let God drive, and let everything else get in the passenger seats. The engine and the train cars.

When I finally opened up to God and allowed Him to touch my spirit (and eventually, my emotions), He began to heal my heart and my case against Him dissipated. He answered the questions that were really on my heart, not just the ones that I voiced, and as my relationship with Him developed, He rendered more and more of my questions null and void.

Why do I believe in God? Although there are many wonderfully logical "proofs" for the existence of God (for by Him all knowledge and reason exists), that is not why I believe in Him. I have found that if you posture yourself as a skeptic, you can have all of your questions answered and still remain unconvinced. On the flip side, when your heart fully believes in God, you can have *none* of the answers and still believe.

When all is said and done, I believe in God because I have a relationship with Him. I have experienced His love for me. God delivered me out of my fears, and He caused me to feel alive again. Deep down in the core of my being, I just believe that He is real. I believe that there is something more to this life—a higher purpose, a greater meaning, an eternal reward. When I attempted to deny my belief in God, my world became a chaotic, tormenting mess, partly because I was stifling and suffocating my spirit. The seeds of faith, hope, and love have been planted in my heart, and I believe with all of my heart, by the grace of

God, that there they will remain.

He is the Answer.

CHAPTER
17

Higher Ground:
The Key to Mastering Mazes

As God took me through the healing process after I graduated from college, He began to elevate my thinking. One of the songs that ministered to me during that time was "Higher" by Mali Music. The song speaks of God's desire to take us higher into new dimensions in Him, and the chorus simply says, "Come up a little higher...higher, higher, higher, higher."

I realized that as I allowed God to lift my spirit and my mind higher in Him, the problems that I was facing on lower levels of thinking slowly faded until they disappeared entirely. The idea was that I could reach such a dimension of peace in God that all challenges dissipated and all fear and anxiety became irrelevant. Often, when I was struggling with a tormenting, irrational fear, my Mom would say, "Just go up higher." When I ascended to a new plateau of peace in God, the enigmas that I previously contended with were left in the basement of virtual insignificance.

In the beginning of the book, I shared how I felt like I was trapped inside of a maze with no exit. When my friend sat next to me and said "the only way **out** is **up**," the idea made so much sense. The dark, irrational labyrinth that I was winding through was relentless and unending, and the only way to escape it was to rise above it entirely.

My intellect alone could not conquer it; I could not reason my way out of it. I had to go beyond my finite rationale and allow God to take me higher in Him. Bishop Smith has said many times that one cannot solve a problem on the same level on which the problem was created.

Although there is a solution to every problem, one must come up higher, to a new level of thinking, in order to find it. This requires more than just thinking new thoughts—it requires receiving a whole new *way* of thinking, a new pattern of thought.

The challenges and complexities of the journey always look simpler and smaller when you begin to see the big picture. I remember sitting in the window seat of a plane, looking down at a city from the sky. The view was incredible—breathtaking. From my vantage point, I could see the entire aerial view of the metropolis.

Thousands of tiny, little people drove in tiny, little cars on thin, thread-like roads. Entire neighborhoods, dotted with brown roofs and blue pools, seemed no bigger than my hand, and large skyscrapers looked like small building blocks.

I thought about all the people in this city. What were they all doing? Where were they all going? From this perspective, all of our daily problems seemed so insignificant. I realized that so much of what I thought was important was actually trivial, and when I began to see the big picture, I felt a deep sense of peace. The world was bigger than I thought, and I was sitting in my window seat, soaring above it all.

I have learned by experience that staring at something vast can engender a certain sense of calm within one's spirit. Many people enjoy sitting by the ocean, looking out over the expanse of waters and listening to the waves crashing rhythmically on the shore. Something about the vastness of the ocean can be soothing. It can put things in perspective and lead one to peacefully reflect and meditate.

Others like to lay on their backs and stare up at the billions of stars in the night sky. The band Switchfoot said, "When I look at the stars, I feel like myself." When God promised Abraham that he would be the father of many nations, He instructed him to look up at the stars and to count the grains of sand on the seashore. God was showing Abraham the vastness of His promise through the vastness of His creation.

When I was interning in Washington, DC, I went with a friend to see *Hubble 3D* on an IMAX screen. The film gave me a glimpse into the vastness of outer space. The camera zoomed out until the Earth was less than a speck of dust in the frame, and then the camera just kept on zooming out, further and further.

At some point, my mind simply could no longer comprehend the size and scope of what was being portrayed on the screen. It was so large, so expansive, that it inspired awestruck wonder. There was color and beauty in the outer reaches of space that previous generations could not even imagine. I was blown away by how big God's creation really was, and all I could do was throw my hands up and say that He is God.

When Jesus completed his earthly ministry, He ascended up into heaven and was seated at the right hand of God. He conquered death, hell, and the grave, and He took His rightful place as the Lord of all. His seated position suggests that He is confidently and majestically ruling His creation. He is above all things, and He has complete control over all things. The Apostle Paul illustrates this point:

> Which he wrought in Christ, when he raised him from the dead, and set him at his own right hand in the heavenly places, Far above all principality, and power, and might, and dominion, and every name that is named, not only in this world, but also in that which is to come: (Ephesians 1:20-21).

Paul then goes on to say that we, as believers in Christ, are seated with Him:

> And hath raised us up together, and made us sit together in heavenly places in Christ Jesus: (Ephesians 2:6).

The Body of Christ is seated with Christ, far above all principality and power. Our current state is one of complete victory in Christ Jesus. That powerful truth has become a part of my personal perspective, and it has changed how I approach the various challenges of my journey. I used to see myself as a victim. Now, I arrive on the scene as more than a conqueror. I am a ruler, a governor. Nothing is too difficult for me because I am seated with Christ in heavenly places, and I have already won the victory.

Jesus is seated as a ruler, and He is presiding over all of creation. Interestingly, the origin of the word "preside" can refer to one who is in a seated position; it is also the base word from which we derive the term "president." The image of Jesus sitting on the throne suggests a tremendous amount of power and authority.

Look at it this way: if one can move aggressively and cause things to happen by sheer brute force, that is one dimension of power. However, if one can sit confidently, and by a simple word or snap of the finger, cause the same things to happen, that is an even greater dimension of power—one that we all have access to through faith in Christ Jesus.

CHAPTER
18

House of Thought

We as human beings are governed by the various "houses of thought" that we allow to be established within our minds. A "house of thought" is a system—it's a way of thinking. Often referred to as "strongholds," these structures of thought are built upon certain foundational assumptions and ideas that form the basis of a given paradigm.

Once a foundation has been established, pillars and beams are then solidly mounted and fastened to the base. These are corollary or supporting ideas that find their validity in the "truth" of the foundational principle. Walls, doors, and windows then come along to complete the structure, and eventually, multiple levels are created. As the house of thought becomes a home, the individual begins to decorate it with various furnishings and frills, until it becomes a comfortable and familiar residence: a fully established reality or worldview.

Every philosophy and perspective can be metaphorically understood to be a house of thought. This includes religious teachings, systems of government, cultural norms, and even personal assumptions and perceptions. Every day, we build these houses of thought as societies, families, and individuals. Our thoughts create our realities, and they shape our world. Perhaps this is why the Apostle Paul gave this critical instruction to the early Church:

> As ye have therefore received Christ Jesus the Lord, so walk ye in him:
> **Rooted and built up in him, and stablished in the faith,** as ye have been taught, abounding therein with thanksgiving. Beware lest any man spoil you through philosophy and vain deceit, after the tradition of men, after **the rudiments of the world,** and not after Christ.
> (Colossians 2:6-8, emphasis added).

In his letter to the Church at Rome, Paul gives a similar warning:

> And be not conformed to this world: but be ye transformed by the renewing of your mind, that ye may prove what is that good, and acceptable, and perfect, will of God. (Romans 12:2).

God wants to give His people a completely new way of thinking. When we become believers, Christ does not attempt to renovate the old house of thought that we are living in. He does not come in and scrub the floors, dust the bookshelves, and paint the walls of our old pattern of thinking.

Instead, He tears the entire structure up from its foundation; He uproots every board, pillar, and beam. He rips up the very roots of our previous mindsets and casts them out forever. The stronghold of fear, the stronghold of guilt, the stronghold of lust—they all have to go. He then starts over from scratch, building upon a new foundation.

Destructive mindsets can be like prisons, and individual thoughts can be like shackles that keep a person bound. However, even in the prison of the mind, if one calls upon the name of the Lord, every chain can be broken. The truth will always bring freedom.

Paul and Silas were thrown into the "inner prison," and their feet were made fast in the stocks; but they prayed and sang praises to God at midnight, "and suddenly there was a great earthquake, so that the foundations of the prison were shaken: and immediately all the doors were opened, and every one's bands were loosed" (Acts 16:26). Today, God is still demonstrating His power to shake the foundations and set His people free.

The new thoughts that God wants to give to His people cannot be inserted into old systems of thinking. The old systems will only corrupt the meaning of the new thoughts and produce chaos and confusion. There are many metaphorical examples that we can use to illustrate this point.

For instance, if you attempt to insert a Blu-Ray disc into a VHS tape player, you will likely ruin both the disc and the player. It may have been a great movie, but you will never see it now. Similarly, certain software programs simply cannot run on outdated computer systems. The only way to properly and effectively run the software is to upgrade to a system that can handle the information.

In the same way, Christ wants to upgrade our way of thinking so that we can handle the revelation that He wants to share with us. Jesus illuminates this concept with the disciples of John in the Gospel of Matthew:

> No man putteth a piece of new cloth unto an old garment, for that which is put in to fill it up taketh from the garment, and the rent is made worse.
> Neither do men put new wine into old bottles: else the bottles break, and the wine runneth out, and the bottles perish: but they put new wine into new bottles, and both are preserved. (Matthew 9:16-17).

Just as new wine must be put in new bottles, new thoughts must be put in new ways of thinking. My prayer is that God will renew my mind until the mind that was in Christ Jesus is also in me (Philippians 2:5).

I want to think the thoughts of God. Bishop Smith calls this "Power Thinking," the highest possible form of thinking. When one thinks the thoughts of God, nothing is impossible.

Christ Jesus is the only foundation for this new house of thought. The Apostle Paul makes this clear in his first letter to the Corinthian church:

> For we are labourers together with God: ye are God's husbandry, ye are God's building.
> According to the grace of God which is given unto me, as a wise masterbuilder, I have laid the foundation, and another

buildeth thereon. But let every man take heed how he buildeth thereupon.

For other foundation can no man lay than that is laid, which
is Jesus Christ. (1 Corinthians 3:9-11).

Christ is the only foundation, meaning that all of our thoughts
must be built upon Him. Every idea, concept, and philosophy must be
rooted and grounded in the truth of Jesus Christ. He is the solid Rock
upon which all truth is established.

Once this foundation is made sure in our hearts and minds, we can
then begin to build "pillars of truth" based on the Word and revelation
of God. These pillars of truth are strong, fortified thoughts that are
built upon Jesus Christ: love, joy, peace, faith, hope, righteousness, victory...the list goes on.

Jesus talked about the difference between the house that was built
on the sand and the house that was built upon a rock. When the wind
and the waves came and beat upon the two houses, the one that was
built on the sand was washed away, but the only that was built upon a
rock remained.

When Christ is our foundation, we cannot possibly be moved, and
the longer we build this superstructure, the stronger it becomes. In the
end, all things will be shaken, but only one thing will remain.

CHAPTER
19

From Confusion to Order

"You will bring order to many things." I can still hear Bishop Bismark's words in my ears. He spoke to who I really am, and I will never forget it. In 2012, I read one of Bishop Bismark's books, entitled *The Order of the Kingdom*, and the message changed my thinking (and therefore, my life) forever.

As I read through the book, I could almost hear Bishop Bismark preaching, and I could feel his spirit coming through the pages: "God blesses order. God cannot bless disorder . . . Father, give me order in my life. I have to have order because God, you are a God of order."

Our God is indeed a God of order. When one observes the way creation is designed and structured, this truth is not difficult to ascertain. God has ordered the entire universe according to specific patterns and equations. He created the laws of physics that hold matter and space together. He created humanity from the dust of the earth.

The earth was without form and void, but God stepped into chaos and confusion, and He established His order. He populated the land with cattle, the sea with fish, and the sky with birds. He planted trees and vineyards that would produce after their own kind, and placed humanity in the Garden of Eden to manage His estate. He even created behavioral guidelines, and when humanity rebelled against those, the entire world was plunged into confusion and disorder.

Having struggled with a mental *disorder*, I know from experience what it feels like to live in confusion. I know what it means to exist in torment and chaos, but when God called me out of darkness and brought me into His light, He began to order my thinking. He began to restructure my thought patterns.

He brought clarity and peace to my mind, and He restored my sanity. From my own story, I know that God is a God of order. His order is not legalistic; neither is it oppressive. Quite the opposite, in fact. God's order always brings greater dimensions of peace, tranquility, and fruitfulness.

I have discovered that there is a major difference between irrational obsessive behavior and true order. Obsessive behavior causes torment. Order brings peace. I mentioned earlier in the book that my mental state at any given time is often reflected by the condition of the environment that I manage. My mind is therefore always on display.

For example, when I was struggling heavily with OCD, my bedroom was a chaotic mess—everything was in disarray. However, when I began to receive revelation and healing from God, the state of my environment began to change, as well. Today, its orderly state reflects what God has done in my life.

In *The Order of the Kingdom*, Bishop Bismark contrasts order with disorder:

> Order is always easier than disorder. Let me give you an example. Let's say you have to go to Los Angeles for a few days and you have a trip coming up to Nigeria. You get a phone call saying your birth certificate and papers are needed to issue the visa, but there's no way you can get from L.A. back to Dallas in time to get the papers there. You're going to phone a friend of yours and tell them where to find your papers.
>
> If your life and your house are in order, you'll tell them, "Now, when you get to the front door, go up the stairs. When you come into my bedroom you'll see a Picasso painting. Move the Picasso; there's a combination lock there. This is the combination: 20-30-40-50. Open the safe; you will find six files. The third file on the left is a blue file. Get that file. You will find all our travel documents and our birth certificates." That person will come off the street, go up the stairs, go into the safe, and get the papers. It's easy with order.
>
> But, if there's no order, they're going to have to step over last week's clothing, find their way with a rowing boat up the stairs, come into the bedroom where there's clothing everywhere. There are Chinese takeout boxes. There's a stack of magazines . . . so they'll have to move magazine papers and move clothing and move old jeans and love letters from the prom nights. And then start filing through your stuff to find a piece of paper. Disorder will always overwhelm you.

Bishop Bismark's book inspired me to bring order to my world. He encourages his readers to begin with what they can see—to start with the obvious things. Begin to pick up the trash that is on floor. Straighten out that pile of magazines, finish doing the laundry, fix that broken faucet handle. Organize everything that you can see, and begin to establish order in your environment. Vacuum the floors, dust the shelves, clean the windows.

This is not something that is obsessive or compulsive in any way—it's simply getting your life in order. Eventually, as I started to organize the small things, I noticed that my mental real estate was then freed up to concentrate on bringing order to the things that were on the next level. From there, one may begin to organize one's finances, or bring order to one's body, or effectively manage one's relationships. It all begins with a revelation of the value of order.

Around the time I was reading *The Order of the Kingdom*, Bishop Smith was teaching a sermon series at Embassy entitled "The Art of Governance" which revealed the value of properly governing and managing one's world so that everything flourishes under one's hand. The combination of these two thoughts, which were very closely related, inspired me to actively begin to apply these principles.

I brought order to my bedroom on a new level, and I did not stop there. I began to organize other rooms in the house, as well. My Dad, for one, was excited because he saw me taking a new level of personal ownership over our household affairs. Eventually, I hope to bring some sense of order to the world at large in a significant way—to address grievous injustices, to bring balance and fairness, and to inspire generations to higher levels of thinking.

Although rarely taught upon, order is actually a big theme in the Scriptures. I used to think that Leviticus and Numbers were among the most boring books in the Bible. How could anyone enjoy reading these books? The dimensions of the vessels in the Tabernacle, the protocol for burnt offerings, seemingly endless lists of names—how could any of this possibly apply to me, I wondered.

Only recently have I begun to read these books again with fresh eyes and a new understanding. Now, these books excite me because I see the ways in which God was establishing His order among His people.

He was creating an entirely new culture, one based on a pattern from the heavens. I marvel at the degree of specificity that is used to describe structures and procedures. God was incredibly detailed about how the Tabernacle was to be constructed, how priests were to offer sacrifices, and how the people were to be cleansed.

God instructed His people to organize themselves by tribes and families, and He told them to camp in a specific order. He chose their laws, their customs, and their feast days. God was building His own society, and clearly, it was one that was fundamentally founded upon His order.

The idea of order is still relevant today. It is not just an antiquated, Old Testament philosophy that is no longer applicable to believers in the New Testament. Remember that when humanity fell in the Garden, the world was thrown into havoc and chaos. Christ came to restore God's order: to re-establish the Kingdom of God on the earth.

Paul reminds us that "God is not the author of confusion, but of peace, as in all churches of the saints . . . Let all things be done decently and in order" (1 Corinthians 14:33, 40). When Jesus healed the sick, He was bringing order back to their bodies. When He preached the Sermon on the Mount, He was revealing the mind of God and founding a new culture. Jesus walked in a perfect dimension of order.

Jesus cared about order so much that he overturned the tables of the moneychangers who had turned God's house of prayer into a den of thieves. He could not abide the disorder and injustice that was taking place, and He reminded the people of God's original thought concerning the house of God.

This same Jesus looked out over the sea and calmed the winds and the waves of a terrible storm with His words alone: "Peace, be still." He brought order and stability to the chaos of the tempest, and He can do the same thing in our lives today.

We must always remember, however, that the order we establish in our lives cannot be based upon our own presuppositions. Instead, it must be God's divine order. Our own sense of order will often lead us down the wrong paths, but God's order will always cause us to triumph. We must pattern our lives after what we see in the heavens—God's divine plan and destiny for our lives. Moses received the heavenly pattern for the Law and the Tabernacle when He was communing with God in Mount Sinai. He then came down from the mountain and gave instructions to the people. Everything was ordered and structured according to the pattern that Moses received from God.

Several years ago, I attended a special lecture at the University of Michigan on *The Sound of Liberation: What Music Tells Us About Freedom.* The keynote speaker was Jeremy Begbie, who was a Thomas A. Langford Research Professor at Duke Divinity School and a Lecturer in Music & Theology at Cambridge University. Professor Begbie teaches systematic theology, specializing in the interface between theology and the arts, and on this particular evening, he offered an incredible "multimedia performance-lecture" that revealed truths about the nature of God in an exciting new way.

Through the study and performance of music, Professor Begbie postulated unique ways of understanding that which is divine. One idea that especially caught my attention was the mathematics of music. Apparently, mathematical analysis of classical pieces from composers such as Bach and Mozart has uncovered specific patterns and "equations" behind the music. In other words, there is an order to the arrangement of the notes within the piece.

Albert Einstein once said that Mozart's music "was so pure that it seemed to have been ever-present in the universe, waiting to be discovered by the master." In a *New York Times* article entitled "A Genius Finds Inspiration in the Music of Another" (January 31, 2006), Arthur I. Miller wrote, "Einstein believed much the same of physics, that beyond observations and theory lay the music of the spheres—which, he wrote, revealed a 'pre-established harmony' exhibiting stunning symmetries. The laws of nature, such as those of relativity theory, were waiting to be plucked out of the cosmos by someone with a sympathetic ear. Thus it was less laborious calculation, but 'pure thought' to which Einstein attributed his theories."

There is math behind the music. However, Professor Begbie noted that when individuals attempt to create beautiful works of music simply by arranging notes according to mathematical patterns, chaotic dissonance often results. Thus, while there is a clear order to many classical pieces, one will find it difficult to compose such pieces by mechanically implementing arbitrary patterns of notes.

Order alone, in the absence of divine inspiration, does not guarantee beauty and harmony. The applications of this idea are resplendent and manifold. Adolf Hitler created a society in Nazi Germany that was intensely organized—and sickeningly brutal. What appeared to be order on one level was actually disorder on another, and the clashing dissonance of the Nazi regime rang loudly and painfully in the ears of all who cherished righteousness, peace, and justice.

The Apostle Paul speaks of those who, "being ignorant of God's righteousness, and going about to establish their own righteousness, have not submitted themselves unto the righteousness of God" (Romans 10:3). Such individuals may be highly organized and have the appearance of order, but from God's perspective, they are only multiplying chaos. Their "order" has come from flawed thinking and does not reflect the order of God. Jesus rebukes the Pharisees in a similar way:

> Howbeit in vain do they worship me, teaching for doctrines the commandments of men.
> For laying aside the commandment of God, ye hold the tradition of men, as the washing of pots and cups: and many other such like things ye do.
> And he said unto them, Full well ye reject the commandment of God, that ye may keep your own tradition (Mark 7:7-9).

The Pharisees were so focused on washing pots and cups that they missed God's heart. Sounds strikingly similar to my experience in college. When I was struggling with obsessive-compulsive *disorder*, my reality was chaotic because I was operating according to my own sense of order, instead of waiting to receive God's order.

I was attempting to establish my own righteousness, and my self-created perception of order was actually inflicting havoc upon my world. Ironically, my pursuit of "order" was producing disorder. Only God's order can create beauty, harmony, justice, balance, and peace. Only God's order can make all things new.

I envision God's order restructuring entire cities. I see people coming together to pick up trash, pull up weeds, and scrub away explicit graffiti. I see someone sweeping the streets, painting old houses, and renovating neighborhoods. Illegal trash heaps and dumping sites will be removed, and they will be replaced by beautiful parks and playgrounds.

Cities will provide quality public services, and elected officials will work on behalf of the people. Broken families will be restored, individuals struggling with various addictions will be healed, and futures will be secured. Thinking patterns will change, and cycles of poverty will be broken.

Education systems will rise to new levels of academic excellence, and students will be given every opportunity to succeed. Quality mentors will inspire the next generation of children to dream bigger, fly higher, and go further than anyone ever has before. God's Spirit of life and love and joy will fill these communities, and His peace will reign. This is not just an idle, fanciful notion; this could be our reality, if we would only dare to believe.

CHAPTER
20

Passion Redirected

Saul, before he became Paul, was an incredibly passionate person. He was highly educated, brought up at the feet of Gamaliel, a premier teacher of the law, and he was zealous toward God. He thought that Christians were heretics, and he was so passionate about his beliefs that he persecuted them unto the death, "binding and delivering into prisons both men and women" (Acts 22:4).

Saul was there when Stephen was martyred for his faith, and Saul was consenting to his death. In fact, Saul was so vehement in his quest that he received letters from the elders to travel to Damascus, where he would bring Christians bound to Jerusalem to be punished for their heresy. Saul's faith was not a private matter—it was brazenly and passionately public, and it could not be contained.

Then, one day the lights came on. Most of us probably know the story. Saul was transformed by the power of Jesus Christ into Paul, one of the greatest apostles to ever live and a writer of much of the New Testament. He went on several missionary journeys, preached the gospel all over the region, and suffered tremendous persecution for his faith. He was bound and taken to Rome, where he passionately proclaimed Jesus Christ to the rulers of his day, and eventually, he was martyred. Paul did not lose his passion when he found Christ—it was simply redirected.

In 2009, Bishop Smith gave me a new spiritual name: Passion. At Embassy, we recognize the power and value to be found in naming, or in identifying the true essence of a person. On that particular Sunday, Bishop Smith taught about passion. A passionate person will be passionate no matter what; it is simply who they are.

God's original intent for them is that they would be passionate about God and His purpose, but if they choose to reject God in some way, their innate passion will manifest itself in other ways: drug addictions, alcoholism, sexual fantasies, or in my case, obsessive-compulsive disorder.

I cannot help but be passionate; God created me that way. It's up to me how I choose to manifest that passion. Near the end of the message that Sunday, Bishop Smith called me to the front of the room, and by apostolic authority and prophetic insight, he conferred upon me the name Passion for all to see and hear. I hope and pray now that every ounce of my passion, for all of my days, will be used for the glory of God.

Back in college, my passion was displayed through various irrational, self-destructive obsessions and compulsions. My mind would become fixated on a particular thought and remain there for extended periods of time. Today, that same passion exists to love and serve the true and living God with all of my heart, soul, mind, and strength. Passion, finally, has found its purpose. Passion has been redirected.

Strength Through Scripture

Many passages of Scripture admonish us not to fear and remind us of the peace and love to be found in Christ. I have included below just a few that I think will prove helpful as a meditation for anyone struggling with fear, anxiety, or any other form of bondage.

Psalm 23
The LORD is my shepherd; I shall not want.
He maketh me to lie down in green pastures: he leadeth me beside the still waters.
He restoreth my soul: he leadeth me in the paths of righteousness for his name's sake.
Yea, though I walk through the valley of the shadow of death, I will fear no evil: for thou art with me; thy rod and thy staff they comfort me.
Thou preparest a table before me in the presence of mine enemies: thou anointest my head with oil; my cup runneth over.
Surely goodness and mercy shall follow me all the days of my life: and I will dwell in the house of the LORD for ever.

Psalm 27:1
The LORD is my light and my salvation; whom shall I fear? the LORD is the strength of my life; of whom shall I be afraid?

Psalm 94:19

In the multitude of my thoughts within me thy comforts delight my soul.

Proverbs 3:5-6

Trust in the Lord with all thine heart; and lean not unto thine own understanding. In all thy ways acknowledge him, and he shall direct thy paths.

John 14:27

Peace I leave with you, my peace I give unto you: not as the world giveth, give I unto you. Let not your heart be troubled, neither let it be afraid.

Romans 8:28

And we know that all things work together for good to them that love God, to them who are the called according to his purpose.

Philippians 4:4-7

Rejoice in the Lord always: and again I say, Rejoice.

Let your moderation be known unto all men. The Lord is at hand.

Be careful for nothing; but in every thing by prayer and supplication with thanksgiving let your requests be made known unto God.

And the peace of God, which passeth all understanding, shall keep your hearts and minds through Christ Jesus.

2 Timothy 1:7

For God hath not given us the spirit of fear; but of power, and of love, and of a sound mind.

1 John 4:16-19

And we have known and believed the love that God hath to us. God is love; and he that dwelleth in love dwelleth in God, and God in him. Herein is our love made perfect, that we may have boldness in the day of judgment: because as he is, so are we in this world.

There is no fear in love; but perfect love casteth out fear: because fear hath torment. He that feareth is not made perfect in love.

We love him, because he first loved us.

Power Confession

The following is an example of what I like to call a "Power Confession"—a bold, prophetic declaration (based on the Word) that can assist the believer in embracing their true identity and destiny in Christ. Proverbs 18:21a says, "Death and life are in the power of the tongue," and many times, by simply altering our confession with a believing heart, we can begin to alter our realities. As you resolutely confess the following, open up your spirit, and allow the Spirit of God to remind you who you are in Him.

I am strong in Christ Jesus.

I am powerful in Christ Jesus.

I am completely forgiven. All of my sins—past, present, and future—have been paid for, and I am walking in the pure grace of God.

I am victorious in Christ Jesus. Nothing can stop me. Nothing can hold me back.

I am more than a conqueror. I am the head and not the tail,

above and not beneath, the lender and not the borrower.

I will not fear. I will not cower. I will not be intimidated. I will never give up.

I am not afraid to trust God. I am safe in Christ Jesus, for He is my refuge and my strength.

I am never alone—God will never leave me nor forsake me.

I am loved by God—completely, relentlessly, and unconditionally. No matter what mistakes I may make, nothing can ever separate me from the love of God.

I can do all things through Christ Jesus. Nothing is impossible.

I am a son/daughter of God—I have the DNA of the Father within me.

I have been made in the image of God, and I am called to represent Him on this earth.

I will accomplish every good work that I am called to, by the grace of God.

I am moving forward.

My Prayer

Father, You are so amazing. Thank You for rescuing me. Thank You for saving me from torment and confusion. You saw me in my darkest and most desperate moments, and You continued to love me until I was guided back into Your light. You delivered me out of my fears, renewed my mind, and transformed my life forever.

Father, I know that You are good and that You desire to give good gifts unto Your children. Therefore, I pray right now for everyone who reads these lines—that You would touch their lives in a very special way. I pray that my story, the testimony that You have worked in me, would be a blessing to them and that it would continue to minister to them long after they finish reading this book.

For all those who may be struggling with fear, anxiety, or any other destructive mental conditions, I pray that You would allow them to experience Your peace that passes all understanding. May they find strength in knowing that You can bring wholeness to every aspect of their lives. Pour out Your unconditional love upon them and heal them completely. Grant them the faith to "walk on water"—to do the seemingly impossible in order to step into the miraculous. And finally, Father, use their lives as testimonies to Your power.

Father, You are the Great Comforter. You are the Redeemer, the Savior, and the Lord of all things. I love You, God. Thank You for giving us the victory in Christ Jesus. Thank You for Your unending love and mercy. You are worthy of all glory, honor, and praise.

In Jesus' name, Amen.

Thank You

First of all, thank You, God, for always being with me. You are my best friend, and I cannot imagine this life without You. You are everything to me.

To my family—God has so richly blessed me with every one of you. Thank you for always loving me and being there for me. Your constant, unwavering support and encouragement have allowed me to come this far. You mean the world to me, and I love you so much.

To my friends—thanks for allowing me to be vulnerable and transparent. I have shared some of my deepest struggles and shortcomings with you, and you have loved me and accepted me in spite of it all. I cannot thank you enough for that.

Embassy Covenant Church International—never in my life have I been more grateful to be a part of a Body of believers. I really feel like you all are my family, and I know that the best is yet to come. Bishop Smith, words fail to express my gratitude for your influence in my life. Thank you for instilling me with hope, vision, and destiny. May God continue to pour out His blessings upon you and your family.

Finally, thank you to all those who helped make this book a reality. Michelle Kim, thank you for the amazing cover design! Thanks especially to Pastor Bryson Baylor and the team at NextLEVEL Press. I would also like to give a special shout-out to each and every individual who contributed financially to this project. Thank you for your love and support, and thank you for partnering with me to bring this vision to pass:

Arthur & Mary Dorsey, Celia Li, Claire Zhang, Daniel McCarter, Deacon Raymond & Marietta Cleveland, Delphia Simmons, Ginny Liu, Harry Yang, Justin Wong, Ken & Judy Cuningham, Kyleen Walker, Madison Pham, Marissa Zhu, Michelle Kim, Orma Smith, Pastor Denise Thomas, Pastor Dorell & Prophetess Tamika Morrow, Rachel Carter, Rachel Liu, Rebecca Lee, Sandra Soong, Sherrod & Bridgette Schuler, Spencer Chang & Maggie Ho, Steve & Shirley Montgomery, Veronica McLaurin, Wendy Yu, Xi Xi Guo, and XinYi Lim.

God bless you all!

About the Author

Nathan Cole is a thinker, writer, and activist. He has a passion for justice and a profound sense of compassion for those who are suffering. Nathan has the heart of a philanthropist, and he hopes to give himself away in this life for the glory of God and the love of humanity. He has been actively involved in various humanitarian initiatives, both domestically and overseas, and he desires to make a significant contribution to the world around him.

Nathan is a member of Embassy Covenant Church International, located in Troy, Michigan, under the leadership of Bishop Hugh D. and Pastor Letha Smith. He currently serves the church as a Co-Director of the Human Dignity Department, which exists to promote the basic dignity of humanity by engaging in humanitarian outreach and addressing societal issues around the world.

Nathan received his Bachelor of Arts in Public Policy from the University of Michigan in 2011, with a particular emphasis on international development and human rights. He also minored in Afroamerican and African Studies. He currently lives in Troy, Michigan.

Made in the USA
Charleston, SC
21 March 2014